CALVIN & HOBBES
GARFIELD
BLOOM COUNTY
DOONESBURY
AND ALL THAT FUNNY STUFF

JAMES VAN HISE writes about film, television and comic book history. He has written numerous books on these subjects, including BAT-MANIA, HORROR IN THE 80S, THE TREK CREW BOOK, STEPHEN KING & CLIVE BARKER: THE ILLUSTRATED GUIDE TO THE MASTERS OF THE MACABRE and HOW TO DRAW ART FOR COMIC BOOKS: LESSONS FROM THE MASTERS. He is the publisher of MIDNIGHT GRAFFITI, in which he has run previously unpublished stories by Stephen King and Harlan Ellison. Van Hise resides in San Diego along with his wife, horses and various other animals.

Books for the entertainment buyer
PIONEER

CALVIN & HOBBES
GARFIELD
BLOOM COUNTY
DOONESBURY
AND ALL THAT
FUNNY STUFF

James
Van
Hise

OTHER PIONEER BOOKS

Library of Congress Cataloging-in-Publication Data
James Van Hise, 1949—
    Calvin & Hobbes, Garfield, Bloom County, Doonesbury and All That Funny Stuff

    1.   Calvin & Hobbes, Garfield, Bloom County, Doonesbury and All That Funny Stuff
(popular culture)
    I. Title

Published by Pioneer Books, Inc., 5715 N. Balsam Rd., Las Vegas, NV, 89130.
First Printing, 1991

Dedicated to sam clemens. He would have enjoyed.

Designed and Edited by Hal Schuster
with assistance by Bob Garsson

FUNNY STUFF

INTRO

The comics page in the daily newspaper is, arguably, the best-read feature in the paper.

Until the 1950s and 1960s, newspaper comic strips were courted and treated like royalty because some of them were guaranteed to attract readers to the newspaper. Today, whether due to changing tastes or the overall decline of newspaper readership in general, comic strips have suffered. In some ways, they have had the very life squeezed out of them. To make room for more advertising and the resultant increase in revenues, comic strips have steadily shrunk in size over the past two decades until artists find themselves hard-pressed to communicate their intent.

If you scan the comics page, you can see for yourself the number of strips which have very simplified approaches to drawing so they may communicate the gag more directly. Some people have dismissed these strips as being overly simplistic, but if you look at the size of the panels the drawing is in, the inescapable conclusion is that the artist had little choice. Some writers say they've had to cut down on the number of words they use in a daily strip to avoid reproduction of a block of words almost too tiny to read.

That's one aspect of the state of newspaper comic strips today. It doesn't mean, however, they are completely moribund. In fact, quite the opposite.

In spite of the restrictions in size, comic strips have managed to fight back in some very important ways. Only Garry Trudeau has managed to dictate what size his strip will be run in client papers. He and many others have endured and carried on, however, breaking ground in other areas which have allowed comic strips to maintain their presence in the hearts and minds of readers. While the old-fashioned, inoffensive family strips have continued on, filling a niche and pleasing their readers, newer strips have elbowed their way onto the page and brought with them styles of humor and subjects of discussion only recently regarded as acceptable comic strip fare. While appearing to break new ground in this way, what these strips have done is bring to the comics page the style of humor and subjects of discussion that many people deal with on a daily basis.

For years, Hollywood motion picture makers were quick to pick up on changes in attitudes among the public and translate that into their films. Television remained an average of five years behind such innovations but it, too, started breaking ground and catching up to what America was saying, thinking and talking with such shows as *All in the Family* (now nearly 20 years old).

It was inevitable that comic strips also would reflect trends in American humor. Newspaper strips remain fairly circumspect when it comes to the kind of explicit language commonly heard on cable TV comedy specials, but they still manage to explore the newly relaxed boundaries and bring a good deal of imagination to these adventures in humor.

Doonesbury broke ground 20 years ago by humorously dealing with the social and political issues of the day. Some people, however, are no more comfortable with Trudeau's blunt satire today than they were two decades back. The same sense of humor, after all, is not shared by everyone.

Humor is a very personal thing. It's like music. What people find funny is very much an expression of who they are, as well as what moves and excites them. Trying to analyze a joke is like trying to analyze a song. Either you respond to it on an emotional level, or you don't.

These individual styles of humor are very much in evidence in the strips examined in this book.

Bloom County, and its successor, *Outland*, have a team of ensemble players consisting of human beings and talking animals. In *Bloom County* these players frolicked in a world not unlike our own; in *Outland* they explore a domain which often as not resembles some sort of impressionistic dreamscape. In a 1989 *Time* magazine interview, Berke Breathed described his strip facetiously as being about, "Silliness. Friendship. Escape. Doorways in the sky. A little girl. A big mouse. Crimson skies. Blue clouds. Liposuction. Love. Death. Trump. Disney. The usual things."

"Humor is a very personal thing. It's like music. What people find funny is very much an expression of who they are, as well as what moves and excites them. Trying to analyze a joke is like trying to analyze a song. Either you respond to it on an emotional level, or you don't."

What he was saying is that he was trying to expand his horizons, abandoning the very successful *Bloom County* because he was afraid he was getting bored with it after nine years. He even admitted to taking a voluntary 92 percent cut in income by turning his back on the continuing antics of *Bloom County*.

Calvin & Hobbes shows us the world through the eyes of a child—helpless in the face of his own personal reality, but who struggles to fight against it on his own terms nonetheless.

Nuts is an even darker vision of a young boy struggling valiantly to deal with a world he little understands. His responses are very visibly human ones.

Life in Hell presents the darkest vision of all, as well as the most complex and the most brutally honest.

Tank McNamara is the sports strip for people who don't like professional sports. It exists to burst the balloon of pomposity that the modern sports world persists in sending up. When entire cities measure their self-esteem against the success or failure of their major league ball club, a voice of reason needs to be heard.

Zippy the Pinhead, an alien from the planet of pinheads, is constantly confused by the contradictory messages he gets from the people he encounters. Often when he responds with nonsense to a situation, he's absolutely correct in his crazed assessment of the situation.

The Far Side perceives reality from its own unique perspective and takes us along for the ride, revealing wonders sometimes inexplicable, and at other times, merely inescapable.

The Angriest Dog in the World presents an equally strange travelogue of modern times but then, what else would David Lynch be capable of presenting?

Garfield, on the other hand, is more in the realm of safe escape, except that the world view presented is that of a cat, to whom reality is what he makes of it in spite of attempts by humans to dictate otherwise. Garfield carries on the crown of anarchy once hurled into the face of reality by the Three Stooges. After all, what's a little casual violence and slapstick among friends?

"What separates some of the modern humor strips from the old reliables is not just that they change and move forward, but that the people writing and drawing them aren't afraid to face their own human shortcomings honestly."

What separates some of the modern humor strips from the old reliables is not just that they change and move forward, but that the people writing and drawing them aren't afraid to face their own human shortcomings honestly. It is truly difficult to sell a comic strip to the newspaper syndicates and then have it become a success. Once that success is achieved, the artist holds onto it at all costs.

It is commonplace to find that comic strips which have been around for two or three decades are now drawn by assistants and often written by them as well, slavishly imitating the style of the strip's creator, who may do little more than oversee the polished efforts. Success, after all, is not something to be casually tossed back into the sea once it has been so strenuously captured.

But writer artists such as Garry Trudeau, Berke Breathed and even Gary Larson have not been willing to follow this well-worn path. While Trudeau uses an assistant to ink his strips, he writes and pencils them himself. And when he felt run down creatively, he took a year off to recharge his batteries. Possibly bolstered by this honest example of facing reality, Gary Larson did the same thing in 1988. Berke Breathed, on the other hand, believed that more major surgery was required than mere distance and recuperation could achieve.

Creativity may well be a spark which can be fanned into the flames of inspiration, but it is something individual to each artist and doesn't burn as hot or as consistently in everyone. Writing and drawing is work. After spending years doing the same thing, even if a few days a week are set aside to recharge, it takes its toll. Gary Larson admitted to being "a burn-out case" after writing and drawing the unique and individual cartoons of *The Far Side,* creating 365 strips a year for several years. His dream of success became a mountain—increasingly difficult to climb each day. I noted this in the strips in the months before his hiatus, even if others didn't. When Larson returned, one could feel the renewed creative energies in his work.

The old fashioned humor strip survives on the tried and true. One could read strips like Blondie and *Bringing Up Father* in the Eighties and they were indistinguishable in style and intent from the same strips drawn 30 years before. They were reflections of the time in which they were first created, not of the time in which they now appeared. This comfortable familiarity is appreciated by some people, but others look for something different in their comics. An element of sur-

FUNNY
STUFF

prise; of the unexpected. This is what Garry Trudeau, Gahan Wilson, Bill Griffith, Berke Breathed, Jeff Millar and Bill Watterson have brought to their individual features, beginning in the Seventies with some, and in the Eighties with others.

They've brought laugh-out-loud humor back to the comics page by trying time and again not just to surprise us, but to surprise themselves. The world around us, its concerns, its contradictions and even its challenges no longer need be left locked outside the studio door. They can be examined and held under the harsh glare of the satirical spotlight so the artist can have his say. There are as many different perspectives on what needs to be poked at as there are artists with the ready wit and poised pens to do the poking. Each of them brings to their comics a view of the world as it appears through their own eyes.

Is this reality they are examining? Sometimes it is; occasionally it is merely their own view of reality. At the best of times, we find we have a common bond with the artist. We feel he has captured an idea we toyed with but never knew quite how to express. At other times, the artist is acting as an adventurer, trying to leave footprints in unexplored territory. He may do this by trying to make us think of things in a totally different way, such as with Gary Larson's quirky observations of strange notions. At other times, the cartoonist may just be hoping to make us think, period.

"They've brought laugh-out-loud humor back to the comics page by trying time and again not just to surprise us, but to surprise themselves. The world around us, its concerns, its contradictions and even its challenges no longer need be left locked outside the studio door."

In the past, cartoonists often played to what others determined to be the audience's expectations. Today we find cartoonists determined to prove that their own ideas of what is funny and what is honest are not unique to them, but rather are shared by many others if only they could be given a chance to reach out to them. Doing this means that those who don't share the cartoonist's world view or sense of humor may be put off. This just proves what we already knew anyway—that everyone isn't alike. That's why the comics pages still offer *Blondie*, *Hi & Lois, B.C.* and other safe havens for those who find Larson, Breathed, Griffith and Trudeau decidedly unpalatable. Now, at least, we have the choices to make; on what to read and what to skip over, rather than the flatline of middle-of-the-road acceptance the comics page had fallen to 25 years ago.

The world has changed a lot in the past 25 years. This is no less evident on the comics page than it is in any other part of the newspaper.

ANGRIEST DOG

Although David Lynch's off-beat comic strip is largely syndicated only among certain weekly newspapers published in certain cities, it has acquired an underground reputation and remains one of the unique newspaper comic strips to emerge in the '80s.

All visuals this chapter ©1991 by David Lynch

by Steve Garbarino

Maybe you've never seen this dog before. You're a stranger to him, too. Maybe you think you could get him to like you by letting him smell your hand.

Don't try it.

Because he would bite you. He despises you.

You wouldn't like *him*, either. He is "the dog who is so angry he cannot move. He cannot eat. He cannot sleep. He can just barely growl. . . bound so tightly with tension and anger, he approaches the state of rigor mortis."

That is how David Lynch's little comic strip, *The Angriest Dog In the World,* begins each week.

This four-panel cartoon is minimal Lynch, and dry to the bone. The scenes stay the same—the first three panels always take place in daylight, and the light always remains "on" at night in the fourth panel. The dialogue is the only thing that changes.

Witness the *Blue Velvet*-like white picket fence with the foreboding smog-spewing factory in the background, a la *Eraserhead*. Note the toneless, blase conversations coming from the invisible inhabitants of the cartoon house, undershadowed by tension and malice in the form of the pointy, black canine who never changes position. Yes, you are *there* again, in Lynch's despairing, mutated world.

As in all his films, this gratingly funny cartoon affirms that behind the pleasant facade of Happy Valley, something is seething inside—like the battling bugs under the smooth sod in *Blue Velvet*. That something, in Lynch's world, is usually sex, frustration, anger, despair and perversity. Yet compared to Lynch's films, this dog is tame, if not just plain dumb.

Though the dog was growling in the mind of David Lynch as far back as the early '70s, it actually was born about nine years ago, when he was first set loose in the alternative weekly *Los Angeles Reader.*

According to Lynch, the dog is probably a male and "it grows a half a year for every year, so it's about nine now."

It is no normal breed. "It's a crocodile and a dog combined," he explains. Of course—a mutant. He elaborates: "When salmon swim upstream they start getting these funny-looking teeth. And they begin to look more like a dinosaur than a fish. I think that's what is happening to the dog."

THE ANGRIEST DOG IN THE WORLD — By David Lynch © 1990

Why did the dog run? James Vowell, editor and publisher of the *Los Angeles Reader*, says he chose to go with Lynch's creation "a long time ago," because it did what all good comic strip do—it amused him. "I'm just sort of amused by it on a lot of different levels—amused by the changes that take place in the text of the cartoon, and amused by the simple idea—a strip that never changes visually but for the change in the balloons."

Not everyone finds it so clever. Too easy, they say. Does that bother Lynch? "Not a bit. They're upset because they wished they thought of something like that."

He is "the dog who is so angry he cannot move. He cannot eat. He cannot sleep. He can just barely growl. . . bound so tightly with tension and anger, he approaches the state of rigor mortis."

Lynch admits the strip is easy to do. Sometimes he musters 12 "scripts" in one quick sitting, and then he's set with the dog for weeks. "Wherever I am on Sunday or Monday, I start thinking about the dog." In the past, he personally phoned in the dialogue for the balloons. Now his assistant does the calling, but he remains "not far removed in spirit," he says. "Some are better than others. I even forget some, there's so many of them."

Lynch says the couple in his comic strip isn't sexually frustrated; unlike the characters in his films, they're sexually ambivalent. Their names are Bill and Sylvia, though Sylvia's name has only been mentioned once in the comic strip. Bill, Lynch explains, doesn't like the name because it reminds him of the word "saliva," which reminds him of vomit.

Bill and Sylvia have a son named Billy Jr. In the beginning, there was some sex, Lynch says. No more! Maybe that explains why Bill and Sylvia say things to each other like: "Reduce free radicals."

Sylvia: Bill. . . did you ever think of how things might have been if we hadn't met?

Bill: Constantly.

Maybe we can better understand why their dog is so angry; it has to listen to these two all day and night.

But really, why *is* that dog so angry? For the most part, it's because Lynch has always wondered why *people* get so angry. He came up with the idea around 1973—"only the dog part, a dog that was so angry it couldn't move. It stayed in my mind because I was curious about anger in the first place and why people are so angry.

Like once you're angry, you're really, really angry, no two ways about it—and this dog is angry."

Then, he says, "One day I got this idea that, since it (the dog) didn't move—he stayed in the same position as day as in night—all the *other* things would change. It worked out real well."

"There's no denying it," says Nance in a voice that could cut glass. "He (Lynch) gets an enormous charge out of frustration."

During talks with Lynch "along the way," the *Los Angeles Reader's* Vowell says the cartoonist explained the concept to him cinematically. He wanted to be able to change the soundtrack but leave the image, the picture track, the same—like he does with movies.

Lynch is still pleased and amused with the concept. "It's a format and it's kind of interesting to me. The beauty of it is that it doesn't change. If they could see that side of it. . . it's an interesting thing that you can put almost anything in the balloons. Let's say politics. You can do one that is far left or the far right, and both sides would be happy. Because you see that the dog is angry. It sort of balances. You know what I mean? Both sides in some way find happiness."

Politics is a bad choice for an anthology, though. The closest Lynch comes to a dialogue based on politics goes like this:

Sylvia: Bill. . . Pete now understands George Bush's plan of a thousand points of lights.

Bill: How in the hell is that possible?

Sylvia: Yesterday. . . on the job, Pete was hit hard in the head with a sledgehammer.

"I hardly ever do political ones, really. I bet there's 10 of them," Lynch says. "I don't usually do straight-out current events."

Lynch prefers despair and frustration and yes, happiness, too. Well, actually, those other feelings make him feel happy.

He says he lost his innocence and gained a sense of fear and loathing when he went to Philadelphia to study painting. Lynch calls Philadelphia "one of the sickest cities in the world. Philadelphia and New York were where I was introduced to the concept of extreme fear—kind of a complete disregard for one's fellow man—especially in that city of brotherly love. Now, of course, it's spread to many places." Like his comic strip.

While the dog seethes, the characters of his panels are "in despair, settled into a grinning-and-bearing-it sort of thing. They were unhappy not long ago, but now they've changed into something else," he says with a laugh.

It should be noted that, through all this analysis, Lynch is having fun. He's less weird than intelligent, offbeat, concerned-sounding, amused. Few people want to interview him about "the dog." There's all those *other* projects he's got going.

Lynch is still pleased and amused with the concept. "It's a format and it's kind of interesting to me. The beauty of it is that it doesn't change. If they could see that side of it. . . it's an interesting thing that you can put almost anything in the balloons."

In a recent wire story, he said, "The humor in the strip is based on sickness—the sickness of people's pitiful state of unhappiness and misery. But it thrills me! Absurdity is what I like the most in life. But I don't just find humor in unhappiness—I find it extremely heroic the way people forge on despite the despair they often feel. Like the characters in (Lynch's film) *Eraserhead*—he's totally confused, yet he struggles to figure things out and do what's best."

Jack Nance was a character in *Eraserhead* and remains a character in some of Lynch's other creations, including TV's *Twin Peaks* and the new movie *Wild at Heart*.

"There's no denying it," says Nance in a voice that could cut glass. "He (Lynch) gets an enormous charge out of frustration." Nance offers an example of the frustration Lynch loves: "You know when you can't get a grip with a screwdriver? Somebody is trying to fix something and they just. . . and you want to just *grab* it from them and *do* it?"

Nance also offers a more literal interpretation of the angriest dog's origins. Telling his story in a comfortable, sit-back rhythm that conflicts with his booze-burned, John Burroughs-like voice, Nance settles in, relishing with good humor his memory of the real angriest dog.

"You wanna know the history of it—the angriest dog in the world? The angriest dog in the world lived next door to me when we were shooting *Eraserhead* (in L.A.), and Lynch became fascinated with this dog. I was telling him about this dog because the dog was driving me crazy. . . and he got an incredible kick out of it.

"The dog was just like that—paralyzed, rigid with anger—and he would have his face stuck through the screen door, looking like he was wearing a hair net. His lungs were collapsed from barking, his eyes were bulging. It was hilarious. He went for anything that moved. When the lady would try to take this dog on the leash, it would drag her around the neighborhood.

FUNNY STUFF

"He would just *plow* his face into the lawn. *Grrrlll*. Snarling. Like there were *bugs* under there! He was an awful, awful dog. He didn't bark—he would SCREEEEAM. Instead of woof-woof-woof, it would ERRRRRRR—'til his lungs would collapse. The thing would exhaust itself. I don't know what kind of metabolism it had—5,000-a-minute heart rate. It was just a wiry little mutt like that."

Nance also supplies an explanation for the conversations that ensue in Lynch's strip. "There was this incredibly neurotic family that lived in the house: a guy who is a kind of a celebrity, who will go unnamed, a wife who was insane, and these two daughters. And there'd always be these conversations coming from this house."

As for drawing, Nance adds that "David used to have this thing with dogs. He'd draw these little rat-like dogs doing things. He was always drawing little things."

Lynch still has a thing about drawings. His more serious ones sell relatively well at Leo Castelli gallery in New York City, a spokesperson there said. He admits, though, that his paintings, which he calls "violent comedies," aren't quite so popular. They, along with his "big chalk drawings," fare better in Los Angeles.

Castelli has never seen the angriest dog, a spokesperson said. Maybe for the better.

"It's very bad drawing," Lynch says. "Kind of a bad-looking cartoon-strip—but my drawings are pretty bad too."

Still, despite the demands of his other projects, Lynch loves *The Angriest Dog In the World*, so he won't be putting it to sleep any time soon. Its maker, who is known as a creature of habit, says, "The dog I've been doing for so long—it's important to keep on doing it."

As for those who would like to shoot it, Lynch says, "The thing should speak for itself. People can either like it or not—but that's of course not in my control. By it simply being, some people can appreciate it."

"One day I got this idea that, since it (the dog) didn't move—he stayed in the same position as day as in night—all the other things would change. It worked out real well."

THE ANGRIEST DOG IN THE WORLD

By David Lynch © 1990

BLOOM COUNTY

On Dec. 8, 1980, one of the most popular comic strips of the decade was introduced. Its creator chose to end the strip almost nine years later. The affection for Bloom County continues unabated, however, and has infected even its sequel, Outland, which looks little different from what the Bloom County Sunday strip was two years ago. Bearing the unusual name of Berke Breathed (which rhymes with method), he continues to produce distinctive and memorable work in a medium which never interested him when he was growing up. That didn't stop him from winning the Pulitzer Prize for Bloom County in 1987, however, and it created just as big a flap then as when another comic strip, Doonesbury, won the coveted prize a few years earlier.

by James Van Hise

"I enjoy *Bloom County* 's unpredictability and irreverence. In a generally brain-dead comics page, I usually find *Bloom County* 's to-hell-with-everybody anarchy refreshing. Opus, of course, is an inspired character."

—BILL WATTERSON (Calvin & Hobbes)

The Comics Journal (Feb. 1989)

T his is probably the most popular newspaper strip no longer in existence. The strip collections continue to sell briskly as creator Berke Breathed's sequel Sunday strip, *Outland*, has been undergoing a gradual metamorphosis into *Bloom County* from the singularly unusual strip *Outland* started out to be.

A friend of mine once remarked that he thought *Bloom County* was just an imitation of *Pogo*. This comment was elicited when *Bloom County* satirized the resurrection of *Pogo* years after the death of creator Walt Kelly; solely, it seemed, for purposes linked to product licensing. But in the collection *Classics of Western Literature* (*Bloom County 1986-1989*), Berke Breathed, in his introduction, remarks, "I can't even remember reading *Pogo* or *Li'l Abner* or *Miss Peach*. I know of them now only because of a period of self-imposed post-adolescent comics education that I undertook after suddenly finding myself in the business. Any proper comics education should happen no later than age seven."

The artist/writer was born Guy Berkely Breathed in June 1957 in Encino, Calif. He recalls a childhood not filled with comics, but one preoccupied with scanning his hometown newspaper, *The Los Angeles Times*, for articles with the words "fire" or "murder" in the headline. "Once, a caption reading "Murderous Fire" appeared below a photograph and I knew then just how exciting and dangerous newspapers could be. *Hi and Lois*, on the other hand, provided no danger whatsoever and, therefore, the comics page went un-read."

He didn't happen on the idea of drawing for humor until he was in the 10th grade in 1973 and did a drawing splattered with red poster paint. It portrayed an astronaut

during a space walk. He had just sneezed, causing the intrepid adventurer's helmet, along with his head, to shatter. Breathed demonstrated such a wicked sense of humor that his art teacher remarked, "It's awful. You're going to be rich." Her statement acknowledged how society recognizes and rewards people whose imaginations are more grotesquely humorous than the norm.

Breathed dabbled in art in high school in other ways, and managed to turn it to his advantage. "I had always been fooling around with art, but not seriously, and never cartooning. The only art that I really had work for me was when I was running for office in high school. I definitely had the best-looking posters and that's what gets people elected to high school government office. That was the only benefit I can remember with my artwork coming into play."

The artist had developed his interest in comic strips by the time he attended college. There he drew a strip called *The Academia Waltz*, which Breathed describes as, "a collegiate exercise in libel and nudity—a sort of compulsory rite of passage for most of today's comic-page artists." Sixteen of these strips are reprinted in *Classics of Western Literature* and look remarkably like *Doonesbury*, particularly like Garry Trudeau's pre-syndication version published when he was in college in 1969.

In a 1983 discussion in *Comics Interview*, Berke addressed the comparisons between *Bloom County* and *Doonesbury*: "It's just inevitable—something that's happened ever since I put pen to paper—so it's certainly nothing new. And everyone's always embarrassed to ask about it. I don't know why. Obviously I've been influenced by Garry Trudeau, but people seem to overlook the fact that, really, in concept and in style of humor, you could trace my roots back to more irreverent forms of humor, even back to Dr. Seuss, I think. But people tend to ignore that, just because I don't put balloons around my lettering, and that makes it look like *Doonesbury.*"

Breathed was very sensitive to accusations that *Bloom County* was just a *Doonesbury* knock-off in its early days. Now he acknowledges the similarities were probably more pronounced at first than he liked to think, although his strip quickly found its own voice and the personality that established it on its own. So much so that years later when a strip named *Hartland* came along, it seemed remarkably similar to *Bloom County* while not really very much like *Doonesbury* at all.

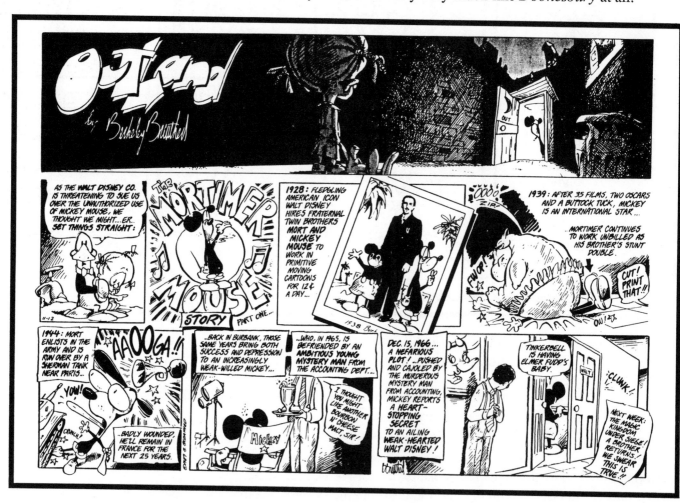

"I wrote the fellow that drew *Hartland*," Breathed told *The Comics Journal*, "and I said, 'Listen, I'm sending you the same kind of letter that I received from Garry Trudeau the first year I was working. I understand what you're going through. All I would do is caution you to avoid some of the pitfalls that I made in not being cautious enough about cutting your own trail, and looking at your work objectively enough to know when you are getting too close to someone else. And allow yourself the influence of *Bloom County*. That's fine. But Trudeau had sent me a rather nicely-toned letter in the beginning and I'm sending you one. Just to let you know that I know where you are, and I try not to be obnoxious about it. But just be careful.'

"And he wrote back, of course, claiming that he knew nothing of what I was talking about. Which is probably how I responded to Trudeau's letter the first year. So, I understand what he's going through."

Breathed learned what it was like to be the center of controversy when he was drawing editorial cartoons in college. While this would not be his only brush controversy, it remained one of his most memorable. "When I was at the University of Texas ,I handed in an editorial cartoon to the student newspaper, and the editor encouraged me to do more." This later led to his first major conflict with his readers, for the more cartoons he did, the more self-confident he became in voicing his opinions in them. "I did a very hurriedly-done, insensitive cartoon regarding the Mexican-American population in town. They had been protesting over a very local issue on a lake near their community which they thought was too noisy, and almost getting into small-scale riots.

"It's just inevitable—something that's happened ever since I put pen to paper—so it's certainly nothing new. And everyone's always embarrassed to ask about it. I don't know why. Obviously I've been influenced by Garry Trudeau, but people seem to overlook the fact that, really, in concept and in style of humor, you could trace my roots back to more irreverent forms of humor, even back to Dr. Seuss, I think. But people tend to ignore that, just because I don't put balloons around my lettering, and that makes it look like Doonesbury. "

"I did a cartoon which was an unfortunate depiction of one of the protestors, and they read it as a stereotype. And that got me in more hot water than I'd like to think I'll ever be in again. I had no business doing the cartoon, and I almost got shot because of it. No one took a shot at me, but if you anger an already very sensitive group of people embroiled in a local controversy by doing something so outrageous that it brings individuals to tears and almost to blows, you realize the depth of their feelings."

In his introduction to *Classics of Western Literature*, Breathed relates another incident, one which occurred when he was hired to draw political cartoons for the *Austin American-Statesman*. The book lists the incident as taking place in 1977—a misprint since the cartoon he discusses involves a parody of a movie ad which didn't exist until the fall of 1979.

"One of the first local issues thrown my way was a busing order imposed on the Austin school system by a federal judge. The populace got antsy. The paper's editorial board got cautious. My response," (a cartoon titled *Honky Trek, the White Flight*), "was a less than cautious parody of a familiar ad for the first *Star Trek* movie. The morning it appeared, the *Statesman*'s editor was hung in effigy on his front lawn. The effigy's papier-mache' head and a clipping of my cartoon were pierced with a toy arrow, a sort of shish-kebab tribute to the two of us. Later, the editor acknowledged the honor bestowed upon us by physically throwing me out of the building.

"They all start out as experiments, as far as the industry is concerned. Most of them do not make it. You'll see maybe 50 to 75 new strips introduced each year. Maybe a handful are going to be there next year."

"That event was a watershed. It steered me away from a career in political cartooning—a career that surely would have been highlighted by more butt-first exits from newspaper buildings. And more important, it revealed vividly that the public's emotional strings were within easy reach via a simple drawing and a word balloon. For me, at age 19, this revelation was like a siren song. I was hooked."

Breathed began contacting syndicates while he was doing his strip *The Academic Waltz* in college. That strip is clearly the direct precursor to *Bloom County* and even included the characters of Steve Dallas and Cutter (then Saigon) John. What isn't generally known is that this early strip was actually collected in two volumes when Breathed was still in college. The first volume was called *The Academia Waltz*.

"That event was a watershed. It steered me away from a career in political cartooning—a career that surely would have been highlighted by more butt-first exits from newspaper buildings."

"I found a publisher. I gave him some artwork for another book he was doing in exchange for him publishing mine. He thought he was on the losing end of it. He didn't think the book would sell at all. As it turned out, his book didn't sell one copy and mine sold over 10,000. . And that's with a university population of about 30,000. It was followed by *The Academia Waltz Bowing Out*, another compilation of strips. They looked like *Garfield* books.

"When I was cartooning in school I contacted a few syndicates and they said, nice work, call us later, we'll call you or something. I gave up, but a year later the Washington Post Writer's Group called, and said, let's put together a strip. I said, fine. Why not? I never for a second considered it would make enough money to live off. It just never occurred to me.

"Unfortunately, if you look throughout my history, I don't look very far ahead. I just started the strip. I got $100 a month for a while, did other things to make a living and considered drawing a comic strip just as natural as waking up and brushing my teeth. I did the strip that day, and I'm through, and I go on. I had no larger visions of what I wanted. I certainly never thought it would make me any money. Money and the comic strips never was an association before. It didn't even occur to me that there was much of a reward materially and financially from doing this thing. And I was compounded with people on all sides, especially on the business end, especially at the Washington Post Writer's Group, telling me that I had no business thinking I was going to be a success, much less be around in a year.

"The statistics of survival on the comic page are dismal," the cartoonist continued. "They're worse than any other profession. Worse than going to Hollywood thinking you're going to be an actor. The chances of just getting syndicated, out of the number of submissions, is like 1 in 1,000 for any one syndicate. They get a thousand submissions before they usually try to sell one. And out of all those submissions that are tried every year, for all the new strips that enter the market every year, one out of 50 survives. So you add that up, and these are astronomical odds."

Odds which Berke Breathed is clearly grateful that he overcame. "They all start out as experiments, as far as the industry is concerned. Most of them do not make it. You'll see maybe 50 to 75 new strips introduced each year. Maybe a handful are going to be there next year. That's how tough the business is. Plus, there's about 250 strips available today, and the bulk of them are in under 75 newspapers."

Although his strips have dealt with political issues as often as not, and he did try his hand at political cartooning for a short time in the late '70s, the comic strip form is what he found most attractive even though he wasn't grounded in the history and influences on the comic strip the way his contemporaries are.

"I ended up doing a comic strip because it was the most effective way to make a point and get people listening, as a writer. I've always had an over-active imagination, and it could have been applied to almost any medium. I don't know if successfully, but it certainly was working when I tried out a comic strip in college. I was a writer for the paper, an avid photographer, and a columnist. I loved the idea of expressing myself in a mass medium. That became interesting to me in itself. And cartooning, in particular, drew me because when I tried it, it was clearly apparent that the potential of it was far more than the other mediums I had been trying; photography or illustration or just writing.

"When you drew a figure next to your words, it had an element of attraction for people that was unimaginable to me at the time. You draw to your strengths. It was quite clear where I was getting the attention from. And so I was drawn into drawing comic strips. I knew nothing about them. I didn't understand the dynamics of a comic strip at all and it took me years even to begin to. I'm just beginning to grasp what it is now, because, again, I'm not a fan. I'm constantly running into these people that know far more about the way comic panels work or cartoon panels work than I do. So it's been tougher for me, I think, to get into the heads of people that really follow this stuff and care about it.

"I'm always amazed when I get these people who care about Opus, and tell me that their lives have changed because of what they've seen, what experiences my characters have gone through. I'm just bowled over by that. Some cartoonists have gotten used to it. It's certainly not just distinctive of my strip. Imagine the people who have been touched by *Peanuts* through those 35 years. When Charlie Brown went through some of his ordeals, there were millions of people that identified with it and felt comforted by it. And that's the kind of power that I'm just beginning to grasp and appreciate. Not that it's there in *Bloom County* , but it's there in an element. And it's nothing that I could ever have appreciated myself."

Some of the earliest *Bloom County* strips are gathered in the first collection titled *Loose Tails* and from there we can observe the slow genesis of the strip, although Breathed claimed in an interview prior to the publication of *Loose Tails* that, "It should be fairly reflective of the second year of the strip. The first year, I just threw out."

So Breathed chose not to preserve the early, developmental stages of *Bloom County*, unlike Garry Trudeau who did allow his early strips be gathered in the first *Doonesbury* reprint volumes.

At the point that *Loose Tails* picks up *Bloom County*, it is still very much a strip commenting on politics and society in the mold of *Doonesbury*. The early strips present the continuing cast of characters, some of whom would fade out into the background over the years. These include Milo Bloom (first portrayed as being in the fourth grade), Steve Dallas, Bobby Harlow (a feminist who keeps turning down Steve Dallas), Cutter John, a wheelchair-bound Vietnam Vet, and Michael Binkley (another child and a friend of Milo). After some weeks came Opus,

"When you drew a figure next to your words, it had an element of attraction for people that was unimaginable to me at the time. "

the first of the strip's talking animals. The presence of the penguin began to add a surreal edge to the strip, and not even his creator ever imagined that this little character would come to be the star.

"Steve Dallas is lifted right out of *Academia Waltz*. He was a frat boy in those days. Cutter John was 'Saigon John,' a Vietnam veteran. He still is a vet, but I just keep it quiet. I didn't have a penguin in those days. I had a dog who was very popular; who had a personality very close to Garfield, who didn't exist then. When I came to professional strips I was going to put the dog in. In fact, he appeared briefly. And Garfield came along and made a huge splash, and I realized that my dog's personality was far too close to Garfield's. So I had to completely write him out of the strip.

"Opus came in much later than that," Breathed recalls. "I used to just have fun with an animal jumping around with the characters' situation, and it was about time I was ready for another one, but it was quite clear there were enough cats and dogs on the page already. Something more unusual was needed."

What the early strips show is Breathed literally hurling down the gauntlet to his readers. The first strip in *Loose Tails* features a Senator Lucias Bedfellow, the epitome of the Washington fat-cat congressman. He is immediately confronted by Milo who shouted, "Anarchy Now!" and hurled an apple at the Senator when he visited the boy's classroom. Milo then proceeds to further confound the obviously inebriated politician with lines such as the following:

SENATOR: Now. . . can any of you little nits tell me which great principle our political system is based upon?

MILO: "Money talks?"

Another early daily indulged in a type of humor few would even consider as being associated with *Bloom County*. Drug humor. When Senator Bedfellow finds a farmer working in his fields and comments on the hard times he must be having, the farmer replies, "Nope. Doin' dandy."

SENATOR: Well good! Good! This is a fine batch of corn you have!

FARMER: Taint corn. It's dope.

SENATOR: Beg pardon?

FARMER: Here. . . take a few pounds home to the wife.

The closest the strip would come to drug humor later would be when Milo, Opus and the gang become embroiled in smuggling illegal hair-restorer lotion, or when a drug cartel makes a campaign contribution to the Bill & Opus presidential campaign because of their strong anti-drug stance. The cartel feels that the anti-drug raids keep up the price of illicit drugs.

Steve Dallas is introduced in *Loose Tails* when he dates Bobbi Harlow, who is clearly his complete opposite. She's a liberated woman and he's the epitome of the male chauvinist. When she refuses to kiss him goodnight on the date he tricks her into a kiss, whereupon she decks him. His response: "Funny. . . sorority girls always used to giggle when I did that . . . . " It made it even more humorous when years later Steve Dallas was kidnapped by aliens, his brain scrambled and returned to earth as a liberal yuppie. This wasn't just a transitory thing in the strip for while some fans expected Steve to revert eventually to normal, he stayed the yuppie even through to the conclusion of *Bloom County* .

Bobbi Harlow disappeared from the strip after a couple of years, along with her romantic liaison with Cutter John. Originally a true ensemble strip, Cutter John seemed to have an edge on the spotlight as he would become more directly involved with all of the other characters rather than only having interludes with one or two of them at a time. Bobbi Harlow was the school teacher of Milo and Binkley, so those two had a concern with who their teacher was seeing and what kind of guy he was.

But even though Milo and Binkley were portrayed as being children, Breathed never really regarded them as such in the truest sense, stating once that he made them children because short people were easier to fit into the restrictive configurations of the daily newspaper strip panel. Thus later, Milo is a reporter on the *Bloom Picayune*, portrayed as a regular newspaper, not a school newspaper. Then even Opus worked for it. So we have a newspaper which employs children and talking animals. It's this strange ensemble use of people and animals which makes the strip look deceptively juvenile while having humor dealing with subjects sternly avoided by *Garfield*.

Perhaps one of the most shocking sequences was an animal rights story involving the use of animals for research by the cosmetics industry; Mary Kay Cosmetics in particular.

"Totally. But note the distinction," he told Time magazine. "With the issue of horrendous animal abuse within cosmetic testing labs, all that was needed was to illustrate the facts. When I drew a rabbit with clips pulling its eyelids open, it was effective precisely because of its accuracy."

Here we had Berke Breathed's very appealing artwork portraying cute animals undergoing dire tortures in a cosmetics laboratory. It was quite disturbing and, even more to the point, it was true.

Right after the sequence ran, Mary Kay labs, the cosmetic manufacturer, announced a moratorium on animal testing and the cartoonist himself admits that he was surprised by that reaction. "Totally. But note the distinction," he told *Time*

FUNNY STUFF

28

magazine. "With the issue of horrendous animal abuse within cosmetic testing labs, all that was needed was to illustrate the facts. When I drew a rabbit with clips pulling its eyelids open, it was effective precisely because of its accuracy."

The reason Breathed was so surprised that the sequence actually had a real affect on reality is that, as a rule, he doesn't feel that political cartoons today have any real affect beyond amusing or annoying someone. "Nowadays political commentary, especially satirical commentary, is usually ink wasted. Eighty years ago that wasn't the case. At that time, a political cartoonist could turn an election around. Before TV, before movies and radio, a drawing of a weasel with the governor's name on his butt went a long way in a public's imagination. Our political

power today is illusionary. A Johnny Carson monologue is today's real influence brokerage."

Another character first seen some months into the strip's run is Bill the Cat, introduced in a strip which stated quite explicitly that he was being added for merchandising purposes. Complicating this was the fact that Bill was portrayed as scraggly and unappealing, the opposite of the cute and cuddly Garfield. Bill was killed off sometime later, and then revived again as a genetic clone created from the cells of Bill's original nose. Bill continued undergoing changes up to and including having Donald Trump's brain transplanted into him—a gag the real Trump didn't find very amusing. Bill is one of the old *Bloom County* regulars who has returned in *Outland*.

Another female character introduced only to fade away long before *Bloom County* itself did was Quiche Lorraine. She was Steve Dallas' girlfriend—an airhead who was Steve's perfect compliment, since he was such a dunce. Imagine our surprise when we later learned that Steve Dallas was a lawyer.

A female character on the scene more briefly than any other was named Yaz Pistachio. She was Bobbi Harlow's niece and entered when Steve Dallas was hired to be her date at a high school dance, which turned into a disaster. One of the best dailies using her reads as follows.

OPUS: "Yaz Pistachio. . . " That's quite a name you have.

YAZ: It's a gross, putrid name, that's what it is, Opus.

OPUS: Oh. . . I dunno. . .

YAZ: I want you you tell me one. . . just one name that is weirder, more totally ridiculous, that "Yaz Pistachio." Just one.

OPUS: "Berkeley Breathed."

YAZ: Okay. . . two.

The strips featuring her character can be found in the collection *'Toons for Our Times* (1984).

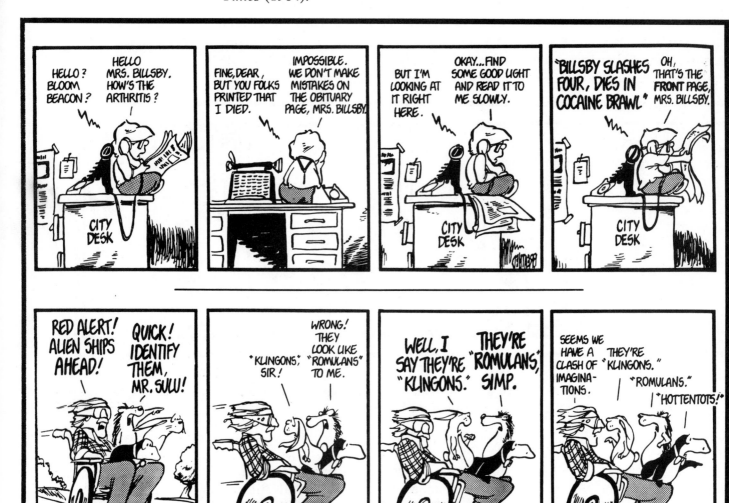

Black characters didn't surface regularly in *Bloom County* until the inspired addition of Oliver Wendell Jones, boy genius. He tended to dabble in scientific impossibilities and succeed, with dire results. When he invented teleportation, he accidentally zapped his father's Jaguar from the garage into orbit around Pluto. He also was portrayed as a computer pirate who was really into his work.

A female black character who turned up from time to time was nicknamed Blondie, but the one who appeared irregularly later in the strip, until she was tapped to star in *Outland*, was Ronald Ann, a child whose parents named her after Ronald Reagan.

An older female character, around for a while before she, too, moved out of town or something, was the octogenarian and environmental guerrilla, Mrs. Lola Limekiller. She turned up unexpectedly when Opus hitched a ride on a Greenpeace ship on its way to confront whalers when he was on his way to the South Pole in search of his mother. Opus wound up teaming with Lola Limekiller during the whaling confrontation.

Because Opus has emerged as a major character in his strips, both in *Bloom County* and now in *Outland*, Breathed finds that readers believe that Opus is not just a cartoon character but an extension of his creator's personality, a fact that surprises the cartoonist.

"If they think that I'm putting my personality into any of the characters, they think it's Opus, which isn't true, but that seems to be the perception. Because he is what things happen to, he is the person that is the recipient of much of the action, and people instinctively think I'm just paraphrasing myself in that character. That as things happen to me in my life, I'm doing them to Opus."

And because *Bloom County* is populated by cute talking animals as well as people, the strip conveys a certain ambience just from a visual standpoint—one which caused casual readers to become surprised or upset when the strip strayed into unfriendly areas.

"Believe it or not, just because physically a lot of the characters are so appealing, the kids who can't even read find Opus very attractive, and they buy the stuffed animals. The stuffed animals are in their room, but when Opus is talking about abortion, it splits people right down the middle, and they can't handle it."

This comes about because Berke Breathed regards himself as having two particularly large influences which shaped his approach to the strip, and those influences are poles apart in style and sensibility.

"If you were to break me down as a cartoonist, as to what my influences were, it would be Jules Feiffer and Walt Disney. And I think that's what *Bloom County* is a combination of. I love drawing animals. I like the character Opus. I will sit around and draw him for fun when I'm doodling. That's not typical of me. I love looking at Disney animation. I love the artwork. People"If

> **"If they think that I'm putting my personality into any of the characters, they think it's Opus, which isn't true, but that seems to be the perception. Because he is what things happen to, he is the person that is the recipient of much of the action, and people instinctively think I'm just paraphrasing myself in that character. That as things happen to me in my life, I'm doing them to Opus."**

they think that I'm putting my personality into any of the characters, they think it's Opus, which isn't true, but that seems to be the perception. Because he is what things happen to, he is the person that is the recipient of much of the action, and people instinctively think I'm just paraphrasing myself in that character. That as things happen to me in my life, I'm doing them to Opus." find animal characters much more endearing than human characters, usually. The kind of things that you can get away with with an animal, or with—dare I say it—a cute character, is much more than you can get away with in other instances."

But this doesn't mean Breathed wanted to change the strip so Opus could become a different sort of character. Even the resurrected version he calls *Outland* still features the familiar Opus fans have known and loved for years, nor has the style of humor lost its familiar amiable approach; what Breathed might describe as the strip's innocence.

"The thing which makes the comic strip so special—people writing to Opus and thinking he's real—I would never want to sacrifice by having him lose all his innocence entirely. And I'm not sure I can explain what innocence is. I know what it is. I could have Opus act in such a fashion that people would stop caring about what he does."

And care the fans do, as the mail the cartoonist receives has proven to him in surprising ways.

"I'll get letters written *to* Opus from people who really believe 90 percent that they're writing to Opus as they know him in the comic strip. Telling him how he has touched their lives in a certain way. How something that's happened to him happened to them as well and how they can better grasp and understand and deal with it better because he did it in a certain way. That's when it hits that those of us on the comic page have much more power and much more influence than anybody on the op-ed page. If the editorial cartoonists were here I wouldn't say it, because they would get quite upset over it. But the fact is that it's that kind of influence that a comic strip has that I'm still coming to grips with. I don't understand, because they have no influence on me. I never read a comic strip that meant anything to me."

But even though his mail indicates that many readers take his characters a lot more seriously than he ever intended, this never affected the way he approached the writing of his strips and he refuses to believe that a comic strip can truly affect the way people think or behave. Because if he did, "I would start taking myself seriously, and that's exactly what's happened to editorial cartoonists. I'll tell you what: 50 years ago, maybe 60 or 70 years ago, editorial cartoonists had real power. Back in the days when there wasn't TV, there wasn't radio even, and everybody read the newspaper, and people got their information from what they were told, essentially.

"Cartoonists at that time really could stop an election. They could change public attitude towards bills pending in Congress. They had the public in their hands and they had much more power than the cartoonist would dream of today. That hasn't stopped the political cartoonists of today from still imagining that they have that power. I've never held that pretense, because I've never seen it in real life. I know people who read my opinions—or Pat Oliphant's opinions—are amused or angered by them; it doesn't change their feelings one way or another.

"Editorial cartoons exist now as mostly entertainment. If you were to ask editorial cartoonists, you wouldn't get that answer. But the fact is that they are now on the fringe of commentary. When they're displayed at all, they're displayed as an adjunct to a story, or as an illustration to the story. As a humorous illustration to the story, usually. And except for local circumstances, I don't think they have the power to change anything.

"That may be the reality of cartooning in the modern age," Breathed continued, "but that's not going to keep the cartoonists from fighting it tooth and nail all the way down and getting extremely upset with an award given to someone like me, who's not trying to change anybody's attitudes." Many political cartoonists were outraged when Berke Breathed received the 1987 Pulitzer Prize for editorial cartooning because they didn't believe that *Bloom County* qualified for the award, in spite of the opinion of the Pulitzer committee.

"We're commenting, we're letting people know how we feel about things, we're picking out the ironies, we're refining them, and we're revealing the hypocrisy where we see it. But I have no presumption that I'm going to change anybody's attitudes."

On the other hand, he's not shy about expressing opinions in the strip on issues he feels strongly about. "Well, I always had a big mouth, and if I felt strongly about something, it would end up in the strip, but that doesn't mean it was any more right than the schlep down the street. In that regard, I had no pretenses about my opinions. And again, the strip didn't start out being anywhere near as editorial as it is today. If you were to ask me now whether I had any business making any sort of social commentary at age 22, I would probably say no, but if you ask me in 10 years whether I should be doing it when I'm 31 years old I'd probably say no, too.

"I mean, we're all getting smarter, and there's plenty of people flapping their gums who have no business in the world doing it, so why can't we? That goes for editorial cartoonists as well. They're no smarter than anybody else. They can just *draw,* that's all. I mean, we all know people with good, concise commentary, for their age, or for their maturity, or for their knowledge. And there's no reason that theirs is any more or less valid than anybody else's. If they can draw, they can put it in print and if people are entertained by it, it *becomes* more relevant, but it isn't."

And with any strip which mixes opinions and politics in with the plots, the strip will inevitably stray into territory which someone will find offensive, even though many people regard *Bloom County* as being very inoffensive territory. On the other hand, the Rev. Donald Wildman of the American Family Association, once called for Berke Breathed to be fired for slandering Christians in *Bloom County* . But Breathed isn't bothered by such reactions because it means that people are paying attention to his strip and reading it, "Especially Donald Wildman. They are probably angry, they are probably insulted, sometimes they are offended, but they read you every day just to find out how they are going to be offended for tomorrow and for the next day. Indifference is the enemy. When I've lost Don, I've lost the war," Breathed observed.

When asked what issues tend to draw fire from the editors of newspapers which carried *Bloom County* , Breathed stated, "You can't generalize. Sex is a favorite topic. This one's a beaut," he said, citing a favorite example. "I ran a sequence

> **"Cartoonists at that time really could stop an election. They could change public attitude towards bills pending in Congress. They had the public in their hands and they had much more power than the cartoonist would dream of today. That hasn't stopped the political cartoonists of today from still imagining that they have that power. "**

where the editor of *The Bloom Picayune* was having a hell of a time dealing with the language needed to properly write about AIDS. This was at a time when the expression 'sexual contact' was used by most American newspapers as a wimpy way of using the sort of terminology needed to responsibly write about the epidemic.

"So I had one strip where the *Picayune* editor is desperately trying to get himself to type out the offensive words and he just cannot do it. So he emerges triumphant with a paragraph that reads something like, 'Doctors suggest avoid using the N word or the S word while the P word with the Y word with strangers of the W word in the H word.' It was total gibberish of course. Which did not stop one editor of a major daily from eliminating that entire word balloon for that strip. My character was standing there with his mouth open without any words. He had censored the nonsensical euphemisms coming from the mouth of an editor who had already censored the real words! I was giggling for days."

"I think it's frightening that the press develops any sort of attitude. As much as they deny it, it does seem to be there sometimes."

But while Berke Breathed's college cartoon strip, and the political cartoons he did at the time could certainly be regarded as being distinctly to the left of center politically, he's not willing to pin his modern views down to such specific slants one way or the other.

"I'm afraid I dance around according to the issues. I get letters from people congratulating me on either my conservativeness or my liberalness, so I can tell I'm hitting both sides of the fence." While it's pointed out that *Bloom County* has always tended to be regarded as being politically liberal, the cartoonist gives specific examples of why that would be a false generalization.

"It's not a typically liberal position to keep attacking the press, and I find the narrowing of our press in this country into fewer and fewer hands is frightening. I think they tend to express a liberal bias in their news," Breathed observed. "I don't think that's a red herring. I think it's somewhat accurate, just in the fact that any press tends to be populist-minded. And even while I may agree with most of those tendencies, I think it's frightening that the press develops any sort of attitude. As much as they deny it, it does seem to be there sometimes."

To explain more precisely what he means by this, he stated his concern about the press in the following way. "It's what everyone's problem with the press is, that they think they're more powerful than they are, and they're beginning to think that they play a bigger role in the governing of Western affairs than they do. I'm a member of the press, and I appreciate freedom of the press, etc., and I can go on about that. But one of my favorite targets is the arrogance that the press can exude sometimes. I find it humorous. Those are the things I think are funny."

When asked about his portrayal of reporters as scurrilous, lying fiends, the cartoonist is quick to point out, "I never said 'fiends' per se. 'Blood-sucking geckos,' I've said. Look, the Russians are wimping out and we're running out of bad guys. If the alternatives are mullahs, drug lords and the press, I'll always go with the ones who dress the funniest. Have you seen George Will's little bow ties?

"I also think that the people's reaction to the press is funny," Breathed continued. "There are people in this country, some of them in my family, who think that the press is in league with the communist conspiracy that's just waiting to take over. I think that's hilarious. And that's why often Milo walks back to the back office of the *Bloom Picayune* and there's Marxists in the back, all planning what they're going to do with the country, once they've got it in their hands. And they're the publishers of the newspapers. So it's a dig both ways."

The cartoonist even believes that this decline in the impact of newspapers on the general public has contributed to the decline in the impact of all strips which touch on political issues, whether it be editorial cartoons, *Bloom County* or more overtly political comic strips like *Doonesbury*. Breathed feels that in the case of Garry Trudeau, this is because his strip doesn't try to soft-peddle its point of view.

"His audience, and he'll be the first one to admit it, is fairly narrow. It's avidly followed by a number of people, but it doesn't have anywhere near the readership of other comics that are in fewer newspapers. And that's because he doesn't pull back. He's a junkyard-dog satirical cartoonist. He's doing a good job at it. But in the meantime, he has lost a very large portion of his audience. He's not read by anywhere near the number of people that used to read him. I don't think that I am cheating him when I say that. I think that he will say that, too. That's not to say that he's not doing a splendid job of what he wants to do.

"He's probably the top satirist in the country. But he has lost that segment. A lot of people I know don't follow the news enough to know what's going on in *Doonesbury*, and that wasn't the case 10 years ago. I think that's more their fault than his fault. But anyway that seems to be the reality today. What I'm wanting to do is make my feelings known or make my points known to people that normally don't read these kinds of cartoons. So my points are often muted and oblique."

In the 1987 interview in *Comics Journal*, Breathed foreshadowed his departure from *Bloom County* into a Sunday-only strip when he discussed the inherent limitations imposed on modern daily newspaper comic strips.

"I know what can't be done on a comic page any more. It's the kind of thing that you saw in the '50s and '60s. *Li'l Abner* was not a gag strip. It almost defied definition. You couldn't get away with it today. There's not enough room for the quality of draftsmanship to carry a cartoon that doesn't have a laugh in it. Like Walt Kelly's *Pogo*. You wouldn't have the patience to get through all that dialogue when you can barely see it. In that sense, the form is affecting the content, and it will forever do so.

"I don't see the comics page growing larger again. And as long as it's as small as it is—and editors resist the notion that they should be paying more attention to the graphics in their newspapers—I see myself gravitating towards exclusive Sundays.

I can see drawing two or three comic strips, just on Sundays. And forfeiting the daily comic strip. I think it's getting that bad.

"I'm increasingly getting disillusioned with the daily comic strip and finding myself more delighted and more challenged by drawing the Sundays. The format is entirely different. Besides just space, the fact that you have more opportunity to express a little more complicated idea and do what I consider real cartooning, rather than gag writing. A daily comic strip turns you into a gag-writer and I'm not a good gag-writer. It doesn't come easy, and I don't particularly enjoy the little snippets where I don't have the time to develop an idea. You're expected to have something funny every day, and if you want to pull back and just be reflective, then people think you've failed that day. You can get away with it on a Sunday; you can be much more muted and much more thoughtful without insisting on a Peanuts-like gag line at the end."

And, of course, this is exactly what the cartoonist did when, to a loud, prolonged uproar from the fans, he ended *Bloom County* in the summer of 1989. But even before he ended *Bloom County*, Breathed had asked those papers running the Sunday strip to please, if at all possible, not shrink it below a certain size. But unlike Gary Trudeau and Universal Press's celebrated contract which demanded that *Doonesbury* be run at a certain size, Breathed chose to go the route of voluntary cooperation.

"Sending a contract to a paper prompts them to do certain things, just like holding a knife to their throats. They don't like to see it. And sowing that kind of bad faith is the last thing we want to do, unless we absolutely have to. We found that we got just about 100 percent compliance by explaining to them why I felt that the strip needed to be run a certain size, and asking them if they would please let us know when they could move to that at their convenience."

On the other hand, Breathed did not try to spare anyone's feelings when he chose to end *Bloom County*. In discussing his frustrations which would inevitably lead to the cartoonist cancelling his own very popular strip, he made the following prescient observations.

"As Trudeau once said, comics aren't a public utility. There's no right to anyone to have their comic in the morning. If one of my fans were to feel he's being cheated, I would say that he is being cheated (in the reverse situation) because if I'm not enjoying drawing the daily strip, and if it's no longer a challenge as an art form to me, he's not getting a superior product. He's living on the memories of what he's enjoyed in the past. If I get to the point where I think the quality is suffering in the daily strip, and I see my Sundays get increasingly better drawn, with more thought put into them, obviously reflecting my own better attitude working with them, then I will make that move, regardless of who complains."

In the December 1989 interview in *Time*, when asked why he had discontinued *Bloom County*, the cartoonist replied, "I'm 32. That's too young to coast. I could draw *Bloom County* with my nose and pay my cleaning lady to write it, and I'd bet I wouldn't lose 10 percent of my papers over the next 20 years. Such is the nature of comic strips. Once established, their half-life is usually more than nuclear waste. Typically, the end result is lazy, rich cartoonists. There are worse things to be, I suppose . . . lazy and poor comes to mind."

Breathed's dissatisfaction with the way his only daily strip looked when shrunk down on the modern comics page caused him to avoid reading any comics pages in the newspapers which carried him, because of how frustrated it would make him feel seeing *Bloom County* reproduced in such a miniscule size.

"I don't read the comics page any more. The comics that I'm really impressed with are the adult comic books. If that kind of attitude was put on the comics page with larger format . . . it'll never go as long as the format is as ugly as it is. You never see that kind of talent and imagination drawn to the comic page, like it used to be, 50 years ago, with *Little Nemo* and the rest. The best artists in the country, the best writers in the country, flocked to the comic form, even in its simplicity in those days, which was far more complex than it is now. You saw all kinds of talent flock to the comic pages in the '30s. And that kind of talent isn't attracted now.

"You don't have any more strips like *Pogo* or *Li'l Abner* or anything with an ensemble of characters. You have a strip about a single neurotic woman named Cathy that has nothing but women problems, and no one reads that strip except for women just like her. You have a strip about divorce only, you have a strip about grandparents, you have a strip about all these different things. Well, they're narrowing their audiences. It's easier for the newspapers to get a grasp on what the strip's about by reading one or two strips. More importantly, it is easy to sell, since you can target your audience.

"As far as comic art," Breathed continued, "I haven't read the page for years and years. The first thing I've seen in a long time is, of course, *Calvin and Hobbes*. He's just exactly the kind of talent that syndicates have not been going out of the way to look for for the past 10 years. I wish I had a dime for every ex-pet store owner that decided he could draw animals and do a comic about pet stores, and they syndicated it for a year, and it makes a bunch of money, and then people get tired of the same joke every year and it goes out. That's what's going on constantly, over and over. It's either that, or the gift-shop people creating their own characters and getting them marketed as comic strips to sell the merchandise. Those are the two influences that have been prevalent over the past 10 years. That's not exactly an incentive for a great deal of growth on the comic page.

"I tend to talk too much about other cartoonists. I don't want to ever leave an impression of disdain for the rest of the cartoon page. Sometimes it seems that way because I'm not very familiar with it and, unlike most cartoonists who are real big fans of the very stuff that they practice, I'm not. I don't even know that I'd like *my* material. Maybe if the comics pages went through an aggressive period of change, I'd take more of an interest. But because of the conservative nature of the business, run by the syndicates who own everybody, they like to keep things at a pace of progression that is almost a standstill. They go with tried-and-true formulas each time. And now with the merchandising aspect of the business coming into being, with *Garfield* being so successful, strips are being developed just to sell products featuring the characters in the strip—which is a backwards way of doing a comic strip. That considered, I can't really see a good future for the comics page.

"The comic page is bogged down in tradition; it is weighed down with expectations. What I find so exciting is the possibility for gentle subversion, to be friendly and dangerous at the same time, like kissing your first cousin hello and lingering. The comic strip is the Andy Griffith of literature. It is conservative, it is homey, it is comfortable, and it is in no hurry to reveal how smart it really is. My fascination is to see what Andy would look like in a thong bikini. Traditional and friendly, but dangerous at the same time, which is a likely description of *Bloom County*."

Bloom County literally faded into the sunset Aug. 6, 1989 and was replaced with the Sunday-only *Outland* Sept. 3, 1989. Characters from *Bloom County*, most notably Opus, Ronald Ann and Bill the Cat, have gradually emerged as *Outland* regulars. A recent *Outland* even picked up a *Bloom County* continuity thread when Opus finally found his long-missing mother. And since October 1989, Breathed has served as associate editor of *Boating* magazine, for which he writes a monthly column titled *Overboard*, which is spiffed up with drawings of Opus, the ever popular penguin. In describing that unlikely exercise in journalism, Breathed explained, "It's about doing to boaters what I tried to do to everyone else in *Bloom County*: reveal the lunacy we pretend isn't there. I, of course, would normally have nothing to do with things like boats, but for research reasons I had to buy one. Four, actually."

Breathed has always respected what cartoonists do while at the same time retaining his honest objectivity on the subject.

"There are some of us being paid millions to do essentially the same thing that used to get us sent to the principal—drawing our authority figures in an unflattering light, which in those days probably meant in the nude. Charles Schultz said it once: you only have to be a halfway good artist and halfway good cartoonist. I know my limitations. I could never make it as a fine artist. Thus the world of cartooning was waiting for me to come along. I have plenty of partial ability."

CALVIN & HOBBES

Everything goes through phases and for years comic strips have existed without anyone really noticing them outside the cozy confines of the daily comics pages. But just as Doonesbury drew attention to itself for its brash political satire in 1970, beginning in 1985 a gentle strip named Calvin and Hobbes attracted attention because it was a new strip which is actually funny! Laugh-out-loud funny.

by James Van Hise

"At a time when comic strips are being drawn with minimal detail and written with obvious punch lines, Bill Watterson's creation is nothing less than a miracle. For all his devilishness, Watterson summons up the pain and confusion of childhood as much as he does its innocence and fun. Calvin is a terribly sensitive little boy who finds solace in the company of Hobbes, the stuffed tiger that talks and becomes real only to him. In the process, the two have become the most entertaining, complex characters on the funny pages these days."

—*Entertainment Weekly*

Amusing comic strips are common and thank you for them very much, but we often get lulled into thinking that amusing is enough and are satisfied with that. When a strip comes along which manages to reflect a common reality most of us have forgotten (childhood), while also gently commenting on the way people relate to each other in modern times, we're taken by surprise. *Calvin and Hobbes* is much more than a comic strip about a boy and his stuffed tiger. It captures the present and recaptures a collective past with bold joy and enthusiasm.

The brain-child of creator Bill Watterson, the strip was the end result of a slow creative process spread out over the five years Watterson spent creating and submitting comic strip ideas to all the major syndicates.

Born in Washington, D.C. in 1958, Watterson grew up in Chagrin Falls, Ohio from the time he was 6. Upon graduation from high school, Watterson attended Kenyon College in Gambler, Ohio. This same college had graduated political cartoonist Jim Borgman, who came to fame in Cincinnati. By chance, upon graduation from Kenyon College, Watterson was offered a job as a political cartoonist at the *Cincinnati Post* just as Borgman was becoming very successful on a rival city paper. Watterson felt he didn't benefit from the comparison. What's more, he wasn't allowed to develop his own creative voice as 80 percent of the cartoon ideas he submitted to his editor were rejected.

"As a result I lost all my self-confidence," Watterson explained in a 1986 interview in *Honk* magazine, "and his intervention was really unhealthy, I think, as far as letting me experiment, and make mistakes, and become a stronger cartoonist for it. Obviously, if he wanted a more experienced cartoonist, he shouldn't have hired a kid just out of college. I pretty much prostituted myself for six months but I couldn't please him, so he sent me packing."

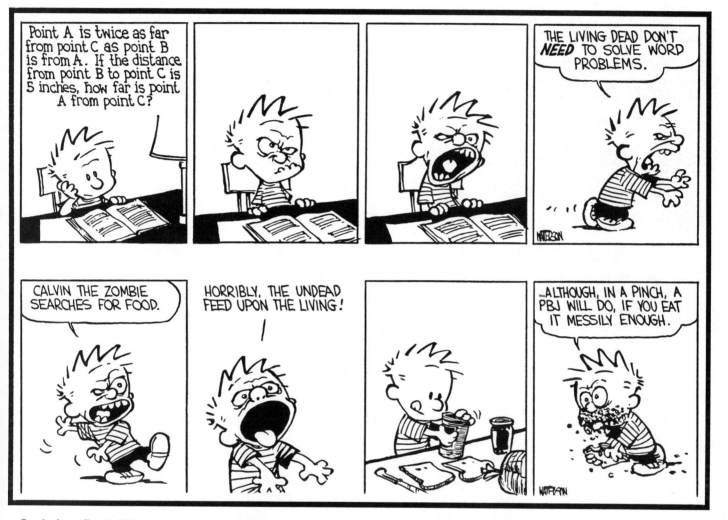

On being fired, Watterson reconsidered his interest in political cartooning and decided to try his writing and drawing skills in a different way. Beginning in 1980, he began creating ideas for comic strips, submitting them to all of the major syndicates, which promptly rejected them. His submissions consisted of what would be a month's worth of strips, to show how the strip would play from day to day as well as demonstrating the writer/artist's ability to sustain a feature. The five syndicates just weren't interested in what Watterson was offering them and he wracked his brains trying to second-guess what they were looking for based on what was appearing on the newspaper comics pages of the time.

"Trying to please the syndicates was pretty much the same as what I had ended up doing at the *Cincinnati Post*, and I don't think that's the way to draw your best material. You should stick to what you're interested in and what you feel comfortable with, what you enjoy, and what you find funny—that's the humor that will be the strongest, and that will transmit itself. Rather than trying to find out what the latest trend is, you should draw what is personally interesting.

"When I was sending the strips out, I looked no farther forward than getting interest from the syndicate, so in drawing up three weeks' or four weeks' material I would hope to show enough versatility and enough basic competence in writing and drawing skills that would interest them. But I lacked foresight in thinking about the depth of the characters and whether they would actually be able not only to continue but expand as they went on. I think that's probably the mistake that many would-be cartoonists make, that their characters are vehicles for gags rather than distinct personalities that can grow and develop over the years. It was a learning process. You can't learn to stand up and walk without falling down a lot, so it's very fortunate that I was able to do that without anybody seeing these strips except for friends."

"In a way, it's surprised me that the strip hasn't exhausted its cast very much at all. The baby-sitter came after a few months but, really, aside from that, the strip has stayed the same as I originally planned it. Most strips grow when new characters are added periodically, and I expect to do that once in awhile, but I think they will always be minor characters."

Calvin and Hobbes began to emerge when Watterson submitted a strip to United Features Syndicate and an editor noticed two background characters, Calvin and Hobbes, which he thought were more interesting than the other characters in the strip. Watterson agreed that they were his favorite characters as well and with the support of United Features, he based a whole new strip on these two characters.

"I had thought they were the funniest characters myself, but I was unsure as to whether they could hold their own strip. I was afraid that maybe the key to their wackiness was the contrast between them and the more normal characters in the rest of the strip. I wasn't sure Calvin and Hobbes would be able to maintain that intensity on their own. But I tried it, and almost immediately it clicked in my mind; it became much easier to write material. Their personalities expanded easily, and that takes a good 75 percent of the work out of it.

"If you have the personalities down, you understand them and identify with them; you can stick them in any situation and have a pretty good idea of how they're going to respond. Then it's just a matter of sanding and polishing up the jokes. But if you've got more ambiguous characters or stock stereotypes, the plastic comes through and they don't work as well. These two characters clicked for me almost immediately and I feel very comfortable working with them.

"In a way, it's surprised me that the strip hasn't exhausted its cast very much at all. The baby-sitter came after a few months but, really, aside from that, the strip has stayed the same as I originally planned it. Most strips grow when new characters are added periodically, and I expect to do that once in awhile, but I think they will always be minor characters. I don't expect to add a major character into the center of the strip. The strip's world is a very small, insulated one which, I think, is more natural to me.

"What I found to be true of the earlier strips I developed," the cartoonist added, "was that I was often making my cast much greater than I had the authority to

speak about. I was trying to deal with friendships and relationships that I don't understand. With Calvin and Hobbes, I don't really think of them as a comedy team that dances on stage and does an act for you. It's a very natural and personal friendship of the type that I'm most familiar and comfortable with myself."

But surprisingly, after initially supporting the characters, United Features turned the strip down. Another strip which United Features was high on at the time, called *Robotman*, was offered to Watterson as a character he could incorporate into *Calvin and Hobbes*, and thereby the syndicate would be interested in taking the strip.

But Watterson resisted the idea of drawing someone else's character and having to tailor his strip to meet that character's needs. Today *Robotman* is long gone and no one even remembers it.

When Watterson submitted *Calvin and Hobbes* to the Universal Press Syndicate, they expressed a guarded interest, but wanted to see additional samples of it. After writing and drawing another month's worth of samples, Universal agreed to buy the strip.

In 1986, Watterson described his working experience with Universal Press as follows. "I send in roughs to the syndicate, which they okay or veto. If the rough is okayed, I ink it up. I understand this arrangement will continue for the first year or two while I get on my feet. Unlike the other places I've worked, though, Universal seems to have some basic respect for what I'm trying to do. Sometimes they'll axe a strip idea I kind of liked—that's inevitable when you judge something as subjective as humor—but they're not altering things, or telling me what to do instead.

"Either a joke is okay as I have it, or it's rejected, and I've never argued about a decision yet. At the other syndicate, I'd hear, 'this is funny, but it's too wordy,' or 'simplify the drawings.' That's interfering with the craft. And if you give a little credit to the concept of the artist, I think you ought to indulge excesses a bit, because that reflects the personality of the writer. Now if a joke is in bad taste or it's not funny, okay, that's a whole different thing, but how you craft a joke is really what the writer's job is, and I don't think that technique should be subject to any editorial constraints, and Universal has been tremendous about that."

In explaining his particular approach to the craft of creating a *Calvin and Hobbes* strip, Watterson stated, "I find that the writing is the hard part and the drawing is the fun part. I like to separate the two so I can give my full attention to one or the other. Writing it, I'll sit down and stare into space for an hour and sometimes not come up with a single decent idea, or sometimes no idea at all, and it's very tempting to go do something else or just draw up a strip, but I find that if I make myself stick to it for another hour I can sometimes come up with several good ideas.

"When I get to the drawing, I really enjoy taking a big chunk of time and working on the drawing and nothing else. That allows me to make sure that I'm really challenging the art, making each picture as interesting as I can. . . stick in a close-up or an odd perspective. This way, the writing doesn't distract me while I'm drawing and vice versa. I can devote my full attention to each.

"I enjoy the drawing more than the writing, so I try to think of ideas that will allow me to develop the visual side of the strip as fully as possible. Some ideas don't lend themselves to that. Even then, I try to make the drawings as interesting as I possibly can, given the very limited constraints of the format. In other words, if I've got essentially two characters talking in a daily, I'll try to put them in an interesting location, have them walking through the woods. I'll try different perspectives. If I've got several days' strips that are essentially talking strips, one day I'll eliminate all background, have it as sparse and clean as I can; the next day try to make it a little lusher or develop the setting more. This is probably done more out of boredom than any conscious decision to do this one day and do this another day.

"The Sundays," Watterson continued, "are the one day that I have a little more freedom with the visual aspects. The fun of a Sunday is that I have more space. Sunday strips lend themselves to longer conversations or visual things or, best of all, both. Although if you have much conversation then you don't have room for much visual. Sundays are more consciously chosen to reflect those two interests."

Thus the Sunday strips offer him the room to pursue the kinds of stories which would be impossible to do in the daily strip, particularly with the size limitations imposed on strips today by newspapers.

"The size issue is crucial to anyone who cares about quality in cartoons," he continued. "To save space, newsprint, and money, newspapers have been reducing the size of comics for years. It has gotten to the point now where cartoons can no longer do what they do best. Comic strips are words and pictures, but there is little room for either any more. Most cartoonists, to make their work legible at tiny reproduction, have eliminated panels, linework and words, and the result is a drastic loss in character development, storytelling ability and intelligent humor.

"A beautiful strip like *Pogo* would be impossible to read at today's sizes. Adventure strips are dead. Comics have been deprived of much of their ability to entertain. Now we have a lot of talking heads and gags that could be read with equal effect on the radio. The visual attraction of the comics is largely a thing of the past. Until something is done to restore the size of comics, they will only continue to get more insipid and have less pull on their audiences.

"To save a few inches of space, newspapers are killing the appeal of comics. Unfortunately the syndicates and cartoonists are afraid newspapers would drop strips rather than add space if cartoons were printed larger, so few are willing to take a stand on this issue. Nobody wants to lose his strip over a few little picas."

Watterson's uniquely individual creativity has succeeded in making *Calvin and Hobbes* one of the most popular and successful strips published today. It appears in more than 600 newspapers and Bill Watterson won the "Cartoonist of the Year" award from the National Cartoonist Society within the first three years of his strip's existence. February 1987 saw publication of the first collection of the strip, aptly titled *Calvin and Hobbes*. This

CALVIN & HOBBES

"Either a joke is okay as I have it, or it's rejected, and I've never argued about a decision yet. At the other syndicate, I'd hear, 'this is funny, but it's too wordy,' or 'simplify the drawings.' That's interfering with the craft. And if you give a little credit to the concept of the artist, I think you ought to indulge excesses a bit, because that reflects the personality of the writer."

45

Calvin's fantasy world is populated by extra-terrestrial adventures as Spaceman Spiff.

was followed by *Something Under the Bed Is Drooling*, *Yukon Ho!* and *Weirdos from Another Planet*. The book *The Essential Calvin and Hobbes* (published in both hard and soft cover editions) featured material selected from the first two reprint collections while also including the Sunday pages in color. It also featured a 12-page color strip done specially for this volume. The color strip is titled *A Nauseous Nocturne* and is a rhyme about Calvin's night terrors, imitating the rhythms of the poetry of Edgar Allan Poe. In 1989 *The Calvin and Hobbes Lazy Sunday Book* was published, featuring more than 100 pages of Sunday strips in color, as well as an original color Spaceman Spiff adventure.

While the fantasy subtext of *Calvin and Hobbes* is on-going in the form of Hobbes, the stuffed tiger who only talks and acts real around Calvin, the six-year-old has a rather over-active imagination in other respects as well. Like the little boy in the old Chuck Jones cartoons who dreams himself out of his classroom and other mundane settings into realms as diverse as the jungle and outer space, Calvin is equally secure in such dream worlds. As Spaceman Spiff, he's generally either crashing on an alien world or fleeing from hideous monsters.

"In the *Lazy Sunday Book*, his imagination runs wild as the monster he blasts with his "Zorcher" is his little friend Susie who, dripping wet, runs to Calvin's mother, whom he imagines to be another monster that he hurls a bomb (actually a water balloon) at. Fearless and in the feverish grip of his own imagination to the end, he imagines himself as Spaceman Spiff in a dungeon awaiting the arrival of the alien king, so a bucket of water sits perched on the top of his partially opened bedroom door to complete his devastation for the day.

Calvin seems utterly fearless when in the throes of one of his imaginative romps, but when real world tribulations confront him and he cannot use his imagination as a buffer, he caves in to terror. This can be as simple as paying a bully the quarter the kid extorts from Calvin as protection money, or imagining that a doctor is out to get him.

CALVIN: I told you I'm not sick! What's that? Will it hurt?

DOCTOR: It's a tongue depressor. It won't hurt at all.

CALVIN: What that? Will it hurt?

DOCTOR: It's a stethoscope. It won't hurt at all.

CALVIN: What's that? Will it hurt?

DOCTOR: It's a cattle prod. It hurts a little less than a branding iron.

(Calvin faints)

DOCTOR: Little kids have no sense of humor.

But the next day Calvin strikes back in a scene still in the doctor's office.

CALVIN: Hey, doc, why are you rubbing my arm with cotton? Are you going to put a leech there?

(Calvin's mother shown over-hearing him in the next room.)

Are you going to bleed me? You're not going to amputate, are you? Are you? What's that? Is that a shot? Are you going to. . . AAUGHH! IT WENT CLEAR THROUGH MY ARM!! OW OW OW OW!!! I'M DYING! I HOPE YOU'VE PAID YOUR MALPRACTICE INSURANCE, YOU QUACK! WHERE'S MY

MOM??!

(She's hiding her face behind a magazine.)

The next time Calvin has to visit the doctor, he reinforces himself with a little help from Spaceman Spiff for whenever he's in the power of adults, Calvin believes himself held captive and responds by imagining that the adults are hideous aliens plotting against him. Paranoia plays a big part in Calvin's life. In this way Watterson captures the feelings of helplessness of a 6-year-old who knows that no matter what he does he's at the mercy of all the adults in his life.

Calvin's fantasy world is populated by extra-terrestrial adventures as Spaceman Spiff. Dinosaurs are a favorite of Calvin's when it comes to having a personal metamorphosis. Once again, this is an obvious reflection of a child seeking to become an unstoppable symbol of power, as when Calvin imagines himself growing 200 feet tall and stomping gleefully through his neighborhood. While many children are fascinated by dinosaurs, since they're monsters which once actually existed, it isn't quite as common for a child to imagine himself as a dinosaur.

Calvin is a true method actor, submerging himself so deeply in a role that in one strip, while pretending to be a Tyrannosaurus, he sees his mother and chomps on her leg as though she is a beast for him to prey on. In another, Calvin is visiting a museum with his parents when he imagines that he has been transformed into a titanic Tyrannosaurus.

CALVIN (thought balloons): His parents, engrossed in culture, remain blissfully unaware of Calvin's terrible transformation. Yes, a Tyrannosaurus is loose in the art museum! The curator shrieks, and Pandemonium ensues! A guard reaches for his pistol, but the dinosaur is upon him and he is messily devoured! The giant lizard's glory is captured forever on film by the anti-theft cameras! Patrons of the arts flee for their lives! Hundreds of priceless paintings are ripped to shreds in the awful rampage! Wealthy benefactors are trampled! The museum is in ruins! On to symphony hall!!

FATHER: Calvin?. . . Calvin? We're in the next room now. C'mon. I think we'd better get him out of here. He had that grin again.

CALVIN: I wanna see the dinosaurs at the Natural History Museum again.

MOTHER: We spent all afternoon there, Calvin.

Another of his fantasy transformation involves the super-hero Stupendous Man.

CALVIN: Who is the mysterious masked man? And why has he never been photographed together with handsome 6-year-old millionaire playboy Calvin? A solitary caped figure runs across a moonlit building top! A crimson bolt blasts across the night sky, striking fear into the hearts of all evildoers! Yes, it's Stupendous Man, champion of liberty, defender of free will! Some diabolical fiend threatens to establish a totalitarian system of rule! Only Stupendous Man can save the day! Aha! Just as I suspected! My archnemesis, Mom-Lady!

MOTHER: Didn't I tell you to go to bed?!?

CALVIN: Oh, no! Stupendous Man's stupendous powers are no match against his adversary! Stupendous Man is vanquished! (in bed) This would have been plenty humiliating without the goodnight kiss.

MOTHER: And take off that silly hood before you smother in your sleep.

Even without the pictures, most of the *Calvin and Hobbes* strips still work exceedingly well. Calvin tends to summon up his alter-ego of Stupendous Man when faced with every day problems, including one time when he believed Stupendous Man had turned back time a full day so that he could put off doing his homework. Interestingly, Hobbes rarely figures into Calvin's fantasy realms involving Spaceman Spiff, Stupendous Man or when he's a giant or a dinosaur.

One notable exception was the very first time we saw Calvin immersed in his dinosaur dreamland. In that one, he believes he's a horrifying Tyrannosaurus, stalking through a prehistoric valley, when he comes upon Hobbes who is sleeping. He yells, "WAKE UP!" and the next panels shows the Tyrannosaurus fleeing from an enraged sabre-tooth as Calvin says, "The meek Tyrannosaurus, victim of an innocent misunderstanding, tears like heck across the prehistoric valley. . . ." In this case, the story and the art are closely linked, each playing off the other to achieve the maximum effect.

Calvin seems to be constantly bored with reality and so challenges it to meet his expectations. Sometimes he involves others in order to maximize the effect, as when he describes what's in his lunch to his classmate, Susie.

SUSIE: Hi, Calvin. Mind if I join you for lunch?

CALVIN: Yes.

SUSIE: I have soup today. What do you have?

CALVIN: A squid eyeball sandwich.

SUSIE: You do not! Don't be disgusting.

CALVIN: I like to suck out the retinas.

SUSIE: MISS WORMWOOD!

CALVIN: Care for a bite? Or were you leaving?

Another time he surprises Susie, who thinks she's safely talking about something unrelated to what Calvin's lunch contains.

CALVIN: What did you bring for show and tell, Susie?

SUSIE: I brought a letter I wrote to our congressman. What did you bring?

CALVIN: A bag of dead bugs I collected from our window sills. (Susie flees)

CALVIN (Calling after her): Best of all, this way Mom didn't have to pack me a lunch!

I could give other examples, but you get the idea. Like most little boys, Calvin thinks gross is great. An example of this from our contemporary reality are the Garbage Pail Kids cards, which celebrate the grotesque and disgusting. Kids loved them while parents were horrified, and kids wouldn't have it any other way. They got the joke; adults took them seriously and decried them for being "harmful" to children while all the cards did was key in to the kind of humor kids already indulge in when out of ear-shot of adults and their more fragile sensibilities. Calvin's parents recognize this and have on occasion capitalized on it, such as when the boy doesn't want to eat his dinner.

CALVIN: I'm not eating this stuff. YECCHH!

FATHER: Good idea, Calvin. It's a plate of toxic waste that will turn you into a mutant if you eat it. (Calvin begins greedily scarfing it down)

CALVIN: Ahhhh. . . I can feel it working. . .

MOTHER: There has got to be a better way to make him eat!

Calvin, like many small boys, is afraid of the dark to some degree. In his case it manifests itself in that old standby, the monster under the bed. This is exemplified by the title to the second *Calvin and Hobbes* collection, *Something Under the Bed*

Is Drooling. In these encounters with the unknown, Hobbes is along to provide support as well as unswerving belief in the danger that lurks below. Calvin and Hobbes conspire to deal with the unseen threat (although not unheard since the monsters respond to Calvin's verbal challenges) until they decide they are outnumbered, whereupon Calvin summons his parents in strident tones.

Because small children sometimes fear the dark, these situations can be identified with both by the younger readers of the strip, as well as by the adults who read it and who can feel the distant chill of childhood terrors that these particular installments recall. While Watterson doesn't claim such ideas are original to him, his approach nevertheless brings some pleasant new twists to an old idea.

"And many of the situations I deal with," as Watterson explained it, "monsters under the bed, these sorts of things, are well-worn themes. Hopefully I'm doing something new with them or putting a different life into them just because it's being filtered through my personality, but I would never claim that nothing like this had ever been seen on the face of the earth before."

Unlike many other popular comic strips, reprints of *Calvin and Hobbes* can be found in only one form: books. Not mugs, glasses, toys or what-have-you. Says Watterson, "Basically, I've decided that licensing is inconsistent with what I'm trying to do with *Calvin and Hobbes*. I take cartoons seriously as an art form, so I think with an issue like licensing, it's important to analyze what my strip is about and what makes it work.

"It's easy to transfer the essence of a gag-oriented strip, especially a one-panel gag strip, from the newspaper page to a T-shirt, a mug, a greeting card and so on. The joke reads the same no matter what it's printed on, and the joke is what the strip is about. Nothing is lost. My strip works differently. *Calvin and Hobbes* isn't a gag strip. It has a punchline, but the strip is about more than that. The humor is situational, and often episodic. It relies on conversation and the development of personalities and relationships.

These aren't concerns you can wrap up neatly in a clever little saying for people to send each other or to hang up on their walls. To explore character, you need lots of time and space. Note pads and coffee mugs just aren't appropriate vehicles for what I'm trying to do here. I'm not interested in removing all the subtlety from my work to condense it for a product. The strip is about more than jokes."

In Garry Trudeau's introduction to the 1987 collection *Calvin and Hobbes* , he states, "Watterson is the reporter who's gotten it right; childhood as it actually is, with its constantly shifting frames of reference. Anyone who's done time with a small child knows that reality can be highly situational."

Watterson lists among his earliest comic strip influences both *Peanuts* and *Pogo*, and in his introduction to the omnibus collection *The Essential Calvin and Hobbes*, *Peanuts* creator Charles M. Schultz states, "Drawing in a comic strip is infinitely more important than we may think, for our medium must compete with other entertainments, and if a cartoonist does nothing more than illustrate a joke, he or she is going to lose. *Calvin and Hobbes*, however, contains hilarious pictures that cannot be duplicated in other mediums. In short, it is fun to look at, and that is what has made Bill's work such an admirable success."

Trudeau and Schultz each home in on a separate strength of *Calvin and Hobbes*. One singles out the writing; the other singles out the art, demonstrating that each is equally important to the success of the strip. It is this vital synthesis that Watterson has achieved so well, and which other strips achieve less frequently. In spite of the space limitations of the daily comic strip, Watterson manages to make his artwork expressive, and five years after the strip's premiere, its artistry and creativity show no signs of slowing down.

Regarding the future of the strip, Watterson has said, "I'm really enjoying the work. I feel the characters have a lot of potential. I'd like to have the opportunity to draw this strip for years and see where it goes. It's sort of a scary thing now to imagine; these cartoonists who've been drawing a strip for 20 years. I can't imagine coming up with that much material. If I just take it day by day, though, it's a lot of fun, and I do think I have a long way to go before I've exhausted the possibilities."

The modern style of humor evident in so many of today's newspaper strips can easily be traced back to a single turning point, the 1970 debut of Garry Trudeau's Doonesbury .

All visuals this chapter ©1991 Universal Press Syndicate

Editor's note: Many newspapers carry *Doonesbury* on their editorial page, as if it were an editorial cartoon, rather than on the expected comic strip page.

by James Van Hise

"*Doonesbury* , of course, has had a tremendous impact and influence on comics, and I greatly admire Trudeau's work. He is probably the best writer in the field today. He can handle virtually anything - tragedy, social commentary, personal relationships, you name it - with sensitivity, intelligence and devastating wit. He has known that comics are not solely the domain of prepubescents. Lately, Trudeau's artwork has become quite daring and inventive as well."

—BILL WATTERSON (*Calvin & Hobbes*)
The Comics Journal (Feb. 1989)

Until the birth of *Doonesbury*, humor on the comics page was stuck somewhere between 1940 and 1955, and certainly none of it reflected with any depth or edge contemporary trends in humor. Humor is very protean and this is evident in books, movies and comedians whose jokes often reflect the tone of the times and are at the expense of whoever is in the news this week. But humor on the comics page tended to reflect typical family concerns exaggerated with some slapstick (*Blondie*, and to a more calm degree, *Hi & Lois*) and existed in a vacuum as to the kind of humor the average person was enjoying on a daily basis among friends.

The only strip which indulged in the kind of political humor previously reserved for the editorial page was *Pogo*. Even this was blunted by having the public figures presented as different kinds of animals in a setting where the strip's regulars, a variety of cute swamp dwellers, commented on their antics. It was a move in the right direction but handled in such a kid gloves manner that no one could ever believe a comic punch was truly being thrown, much less landing with much impact. While today *Pogo* is regarded as being a very historically significant strip, it is so only in the narrowest of contexts. It gave other people ideas, primarily in regard to wanting to push that style of humor to the edge where it would truly deliver the goods.

The first daily newspaper strip to do this was *Doonesbury* , and when it first appeared in 1970, it delivered a jolt to the complacent humor that people were accustomed to reading in their newspapers. This was at a time when the underground comics of the late Sixties had been kicking down barriers and going where no comic books had gone before. While *Doonesbury* wasn't as outrageous and extreme as *Zap Comics* and other champions of the counter culture cartoonists, it seemed so in comparison to everything else on the average newspaper comic page. It thrived on this "extreme in comparison" approach.

Like the single panel cartoons found on the editorial page, *Doonesbury* took a stand on issues of the day, both political and sociological. It dealt with the same every day concerns that most people were talking about and, by taking a stand, it annoyed all those who held opposing views; but then editorial cartoons had always done this. In the context of the editorial page, it was just one more opinion among many others. On the comics page, *no one* had an opinion about anything of moment, and for someone to do so came as quite a shock to some people. They acted

like someone had snuck up on them with a club or spit in their soup, a comparison the young creator of *Doonesbury* would probably agree with as it was his intention to say something rather than merely tell safe jokes.

Doonesbury first appeared under the title *Bull Tales* in Yale University's student newspaper. It was spotted there by Universal Press syndicator Jim Andrews. As a new syndicate, Universal was open to both new talent and new ideas, and John McMeel, president of UPS, wanted to bring new ideas to the too-often staid comics page. On s*Bull Tales* , McMeel signed Trudeau to a contract and editor Jim Andrews worked with the artist/writer to reshape his strip for national syndication. It debuted in October 1970, when Garry Trudeau was just 21. He continued to do the strip and attend college and became a graduate of the Yale School of Art.

In describing what changes *Bull Tales* went through to become *Doonesbury* , in a 1971 interview with Jay Maeder, Trudeau explained, "I had the same characters. It was a football strip, first of all, and later focused on the sexual episodes of Michael Doonesbury , and this is what got cut. This seems to be the touchiest subject of them all. And, you know, I get letters from mid-western housewives saying that their children shouldn't be reading this stuff."

Regarding whether he was deliberately trying to be provocative in the strip from the beginning, Trudeau said, "I thought it was pretty tame by the time they got around to cutting out all the stuff I'd been doing. Editors, on the other hand, thought it was very subversive and very avant-garde. I think the comics page is probably one of the most conservative pages in any newspaper. Editors have a huge responsibility with the comics page. Next to the headlines, it's the most widely read part of the paper, which is kind of extraordinary when you think about it. But essentially the comics page is a tranquilizer. Readers don't want to be provoked or irritated. If they do, they'll turn to the editorial page and read Feiffer.

"The primary role of the cartoonist is entertainer. Social commentary is sort of secondary. But I don't think I could get away with some of the things I get away with if the strip didn't make people laugh. I mean, like I say, a lot of editors were really scared by the strip and they really thought it was revolutionary. But you know, it's nothing at all compared to what's on television or even the rest of the paper. It's this double-standard they've got about what they can put on the front page. And to say, 'Good Lord, the children will read this!' is somewhat ludicrous because the kids will go to the TV and turn on *Mod Squad*. You know, it's a little irrational."

Regarding the way comic strips in the past have dealt with the kinds of issues and characters Trudeau deals with daily in *Doonesbury* , he observed, "They get around to talking about things five years after they happen. Like (Charles) Schultz

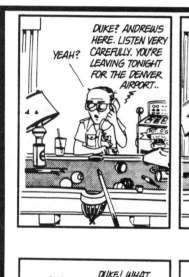

introduced one of his little black characters a fashionable five years after the Kerner Commission, almost as if somebody had said, okay, you can do your thing now."

In 1971, some newspaper comic strips were beginning to feature black characters more prominently, and of these Trudeau said, "I'm following some of them. *Friday Foster* is a new one which is pretty good. Unfortunately, Friday Foster is kind of like Diana Ross: she's palatable to the white public. She's hardly an Afro. Lt.

Flap in *Beetle Bailey*, he's another one. I've talked to syndicate people and some of them think Lt. Flap is the most revolutionary thing to happen in comics in 20 years. I don't really agree. I think Flap is very two-dimensional; a modern stereotype. You know, he's a finger-clicking brother. Instead of the 50s civil rights gray suit, now you've got the hip black Afro, and I don't think it's any more real."

Even though the early *Doonesbury* hit the comics page with the impact of an underground comic book, Trudeau admitted his influences were much more traditional. Regarding which strips he feels have contributed something substantial to newspaper comics, he said, "Well, Schultz has contributed the most, obviously, simply for bringing such total humanity to the strip. And Feiffer. Both had influenced me a lot. Walt Kelly is an old master."

A student of comic strips both old and new, Trudeau also speaks highly of Winsor McCay's *Little Nemo In Slumberland*. In discussing the important of that strip and its special gift for fantasy, Trudeau wrote, "A flight of fantasy, whether in dream or daydream, is no mere sleight of mind. But only children will accept it as being equally as profound as the arbitrary state of awareness we are taught to regard as reality, and hence, only they are nurtured by it.

"Later, of course, many of us comprehend our self-imposed poverty and try to double-back, but the bread crumbs are always missing and our failures are immense. A true belief in the validity of non-ordinary reality, with all that it can teach us, seems beyond the capabilities of every practicing adult, with the possible exception of Frederico Fellini."

The earliest days of the strip, now preserved in the book *The Doonesbury Chronicles* (from which the above quote about Winsor McCay is taken), show a strip with linework which is a bit crude and shaky compared to what we're used to seeing today. The early strips are pretty bare, art-wise, and still had not yet discovered the concept of a background. Even foreground details are sparse. The early strips concentrated on introducing the characters, and in spite

"The primary role of the cartoonist is entertainer. Social commentary is sort of secondary. But I don't think I could get away with some of the things I get away with if the strip didn't make people laugh. I mean, like I say, a lot of editors were really scared by the strip and they really thought it was revolutionary. But you know, it's nothing at all compared to what's on television or even the rest of the paper."

of its hell-raising reputation, it eased itself into American households rather than landing on the comics page with the impact of a bombshell.

The first weeks of the strip are actually very commonplace in their style of humor and didn't look at all out of place in comparison to the other comic strips of the day. Michael Doonesbury , college student, and his football player roommate, B.D., are the first characters introduced and their odd couple personalities form the basis for the gags. The third week of the strip introduced the student radical Mark Slackmeyer, certainly not your typical denizen of the comics page. Mark had scruffy hair, a moustache and five o'clock shadow. The first three strips introducing him dealt with him taking over the house of the president of the university.

In between the jokes were comments about ROTC on campus, showing that political ideas were working their way into the strip. Previously the only student radicals on the comics page were in distinctly derogatory contexts. The most memorable was in *The Jackson Twins* (a strip which was humorous on Sundays but a soap opera on weekdays). In the late 60s, it had a weekday storyline concerning a mythical radical student group which went by the acronym BAG (for Burn America to the Ground) that The Jackson Twins exposed for good and all. Seeing a hippie radical as one of a comic strip's protagonists was a distinctly unexpected move, and in 1970 was doubtless considered "daring" by industry insiders.

In those early weeks of the strip, the political commentary remained confined to the days (two to three at a time) when Mark Slackmeyer appeared in the strip, but it would soon start to branch out. Black characters with names like Calvin and Rufus began to appear in the strip and they talked and acted like real black people as opposed to whites with dark skin. Calvin was another student radical while Rufus was a youth Mike Doonesbury was hired to tutor.

The character of B.D., first just a student and football player, soon emerged as the resident conservative among the main character. His trademark was, and remains, the fact that he always wears a football helmet (even in the shower, we assume). When B.D. attends ROTC camp, he demonstrates a real enthusiasm on the machine gun target range.

The strip really began to pick up an edge when it introduced drugs as a subject of discussion. It began with the daily in which Mark, home from college, is introduced to his mother's bridge guests and he says, "Hi, girls. My name's Mark. I smoke marijuana," whereupon the women either faint or scream while Mark grins in amusement at their antics. Drugs presented as an object of casual discussion and easy humor was unknown in normal comics up until this time. While it met with a lot of negative reaction, the strip merely dramatized the widely divergent views of drugs held in society and as reflected in articles throughout the rest of the newspaper in which the strip appeared.

The strip began to receive flack early, although in the earliest days Trudeau was more casual in his reactions to it and often worked with Universal Press Syndicate to keep from going too far.

While one couldn't say the strip was truly advocating drug use, by portraying it in a casual manner which wasn't definitely non-negative, it could certainly carry the impression that it *was* advocating it. When a second character, Zonker Harris, was introduced a week later, and he was actually shown smoking marijuana, the very different nature o*Doonesbury* was established once and for all. What Trudeau actually did was introduce a group of characters who formed a cross-section of college-age people. In real life that would include some people who engaged in casual drug use, which in those less enlightened times was considered by them to be harmless. *Doonesbury* was the only comic strip of 1970 which truly reflected the times in which it appeared, unlike other contemporary strips of the day which reflected a time more familiar to people in 1960.

While the strip always had a distinctly liberal slant, it was not above poking fun at the left side of the political spectrum as well. The Rev. Scott Sloan was a character common to the '60s. He was a priest who spent all his time fighting for liberal causes but, in so doing, had no real life of his own and no longer knew how to communicate with people on a personal level except with cliches. He even referred to himself as "the fighting young priest who can talk to the young."

Says Trudeau, "The interesting thing is that I seem to keep people guessing as to what my politics are, and I think that's the way it should be. I think it would be a mistake to impose my politics on anyone. If anything, the success of the strip has been its understanding of any point of view, which is why I have a spectrum of characters from radicals to hardhats. I can hit kind of anything."

Other characters soon to appear included Joanie Caucus, a woman who ran away from a stifling marriage, including her children, in order to start her life over again. Comic strips tended not to portray the American family as dysfunctional in any way, which ignored the fact that most newspaper readers were suffering in families which failed to approach the ideal favored by TV sitcoms.

Another character who became a fast favorite is Uncle Duke, a fast-talking gonzo journalist for *Rolling Stone* magazine. Duke was clearly based on journalist Hunter Thompson, a man who Trudeau to this day has never met. Introduced as the uncle of character Zonker Harris, Duke accepts a $3,000 speaking engagement, provided he's paid upon arrival in tens and twenties, much of which he quickly blows on il-

legal prescription drugs and booze. Duke arrives at the lecture late and completely wasted, a state of mind he would occupy during many of his appearances in the strip.

Duke also is a gun enthusiast, but not the kind the National Rifle Association would ever want speaking on its behalf (although he did just that in one series in which Duke appears before a congressional hearing on gun control). Since Hunter Thompson is known for his hyperbole, one doesn't know whether he ever seriously meant the threat he made about the cartoonist when he was quoted as saying, "If I ever catch that little . . . I'll tear his lungs out." The fact that the threat was made some 15 years ago leads one to believe it was part of Thompson's carefully orchestrated public image.

Needless to say, the strip began to receive flack early, although in the earliest days Trudeau was more casual in his reactions to it and often worked with Universal Press Syndicate to keep from going too far. When asked whether there were occasions when his editors found his work unacceptable, Trudeau remarked, "Oh, all the time. I enjoy working at the level at which I'm working. I don't feel censored. But there are times when the greater wisdom that these guys have acquired prevails, and when I will bow to someone's wishes on a subject. Things like how many episodes on a certain subject I can use in six weeks. They have a better idea of what that's all about than I do. Essentially we agree on just about everything.

"Usually when I do get slapped on the wrist, it's not from the syndicate, it's from one of the papers. We've gotten into a lot of trouble on the west coast. The *Los Angeles Times* wasn't very happy about the sequence I did on a Black Panther trial. It was sort of heavy for most of their readership."

Trudeau doesn't criticize editors who decide to pull a story they deem questionable. "That's not censorship; it's editing. Each makes a daily judgment about community standards." He does tend to be surprised by the fact that some papers will be outraged by one story while others will have no problems with the same set of strips. In 1973, when one strip featured Mark Slackmeyer gleefully declaring Watergate conspirator John Mitchell "Guilty, guilty, guilty, guilty!," many papers refused to publish it. An equally hard-hitting series on Oliver North in 1987 ran without any controversy whatsoever.

When he began the strip, due to the concerns of the UPS syndicate over including political material, Trudeau sent what he terms an "inane questionnaire" to newspaper editors to see what subjects they would consider appropriate or inappropriate. The comment that truly showed him the way was from an editor who said, "It has nothing to do with subjects, it's how you execute it." Said Trudeau, that observation, "opened up a world to me, and I felt if you bring a certain amount of taste and judgment there's *nothing* that can't be addressed in comic strips."

How Trudeau views including hard political commentary in a comic strip was best expressed by his reaction to the strips he did in 1980, when John Anderson was running for President. When he was accused of shamelessly promoting Anderson in his strip, Trudeau's reaction was, "Puzzlement. Anyone dumb enough to get his political information from a comic strip deserves what he gets at the polls. The Anderson strips were perceived as kindly, and thus an endorsement.

"The candidate's own view of the cartoon connection changed from week to week. At first he was disturbed, then he started quoting the strip in every speech. Later, both he and his campaign manager repudiated it. It made it very hard for the public to keep abreast of the impact I was supposed to be having. In the end, I think I only swayed about three or four million votes, although which way I can't be sure."

The political content in *Doonesbury* cannot be denied and has remained undiminished over the years. Looking back over the early strips, they actually serve as a sort of time capsule and a document of the times, capturing the mood that was in the air, particularly during the time of the Watergate scandal. Some of Trudeau's most incisive commentary can be found in these strips in both the writing and the art. Richard Nixon himself never appeared in the strip; Trudeau used an image of the White House to represent the presidency.

As the Watergate scandal dragged on and the pressure on the presidency increased in the light of more and more disclosures, Trudeau drew the White House as a building under siege, first with a fence around it, then a tank patrolling the grounds, and finally with a wall so high it hide the White House behind it as the Watergate Hearings began. The strip showing the wall being built has quotes behind it of Nixon telling his aides to "stonewall" and these quotes are directly from the transcript of Nixon's secret oval office tapes.

> **"Usually when I do get slapped on the wrist, it's not from the syndicate, it's from one of the papers. We've gotten into a lot of trouble on the west coast. The Los Angeles Times wasn't very happy about the sequence I did on a Black Panther trial. It was sort of heavy for most of their readership."**

It's hard to believe all that was more than 16 years ago, but because so much time has passed, the historical context of the incident is more pronounced, particularly in light of how well Nixon has weathered the disgrace while his aides all went on to write individual books about the incident. The time seems distant now, but Trudeau's strips capture the intensity of concern America felt at the time over the disclosures of a petty break-in going all the way to the White House. They capture particularly well the frantic attempts being made to try to shore up the President's public image.

Events were moving fast in those days and not everyone even remembers that just days before his resignation, Nixon was still maintaining that he would never resign, no matter what happened. It was a crucial time in our recent history about which much has been written. By looking at the political cartoons of the time, we can recapture the day-to-day anxieties of the period, although the the detailed underpinnings of it all and the complex personalities involved certainly aren't captured not could they be in such a format. The tenor of the time is what these strips reflect.

Trudeau often found unusual points to focus on in a political crisis, and Watergate was no exception. In a 1974 strip where Mark Slackmeyer and Mike Doonesbury are doing a radio broadcast, the following observations are offered.

MARK: For obvious reasons, there can be no presentation of the award for Best Female Conspirator. The absence of Watergate women is the subject of Michael Doonesbury 's analysis.

MIKE: Because of sexist policies in the White House, there were no women in on the decision-making process of the cover-up. While Ms. Woods and Ms. Harmony did their parts, they were not in real positions of power. We recognize the prevailing belief that women are "unable to keep a secret," but in our judgment, this does not justify withholding from women their equal right to obstruct justice! We, the management of WBBY, deplore this situation.

MARK: We invite your comments, too.

When President Nixon resigned, Trudeau's sole comment on the resignation was a daily strip without dialogue showing the wall around the White House being chipped down and carted away, leaving the White House in a pastoral setting with birds, tulips and a butterfly while the sun broke through the clouds behind it. Without a word of comment, it said it all.

These strips were no doubt instrumental in Garry Trudeau being the first comic-strip artist to win the Pulitzer Prize, which occurred in 1975. The Editorial Cartoonists' Society protested on behalf of its members (of which, ironically, Trudeau was one, although his traditional editorial cartoons appeared with occasional articles rather than on a daily editorial page like the other members) and actually condemned the Pulitzer committee. Once the Pulitzer committee assured Trudeau the award was irrevocable, he supported the resolution adopted against him.

In the book *The People's Doonesbury* (1981), in an interview with Trudeau, when asked about what it was like to win the coveted award, he replied, "What's to tell. . . it's the classiest award in America. No dinner, no acceptance speeches, no TV show. They just call you up and say, 'Good going, the check is in the mail.' Everybody in my neighborhood was very proud of me."

All the awards in the world, however, can't stop a writer from feeling tired and stagnant. When Trudeau feared his strip was heading for the kind of cold complacency which other long-time on-going strips had fallen into, he set a precedent in 1983 by taking a 21-month sabbatical from *Doonesbury* to recharge himself creatively.

This was a working vacation as he shaped a Broadway musical adaptation of *Doonesbury* with Elizabeth Swados and wrote a sitcom pilot called *Club Fed* about white collar criminals, which didn't sell. He also crafted unproduced screenplays about right-wing activists and campaign reporters. His most successful enterprises during his period away from the strip were a 1984 anti-Reagan musical revue called *Rap Master Ronnie* and *Tanner*, an HBO series about the travails of a mythical candidate running for President in 1988.

When Trudeau returned with the strip in 1984, just in time to get in his licks on the Presidential campaign, he unveiled a strip which had matured along with its characters. Michael Doonesbury was married and working as a Madison Avenue advertising artist. Joanie Caucus had graduated from law school and was working in the office of congresswoman Lacey Davenport. Mark Slackmeyer had become a radio talk show host. B.D. was, well, still B.D. His girlfriend, Boopsie, was working as an actress in Hollywood and he was her business manager, not unlike the real-life team of John and Bo Derek.

In real life some people never change, so Zonker was still a hippie and completely oblivious to the fact that he was now of another era. Uncle Duke was still getting himself involved in shady political deals, including becoming the ambassador to whatever was the latest country the United States had been forced to save from itself.

In the past, the content of the strip had been its biggest headache to some editors. When Trudeau brought it back in 1984, he made the *size* of the strip a subject of controversy. Like any true student of comics, Trudeau had been dismayed at the policies of newspaper editors nationwide who gradually had been shrinking the size of comic strips over the years. Artists were forced to simplify their styles in order to guarantee they would show up when reproduced in such tiny sizes. Sunday pages, which always had been at least a half page in size, now commonly ran a third of a page (and sometimes even smaller). The hardest hit had been the daily strips, which had been shrunk to fit other features on the comics page, like horoscopes, crossword puzzles and advice columns.

Trudeau convinced Universal Press Syndicate to hold the line and insist that any paper which signed up to carry *Doonesbury* had to run it at a minimum size, which

would make it noticeably larger than any other strip on the comics page. Editors fussed and fumed but grudgingly accepted the demand. Some tried to run it in the smaller size, hoping they wouldn't get caught, but eventually were brought into line as UPS stated that it would pull the strip from any paper which failed to live up to its contract.

In the six years since Trudeau re-introduced his strip, other dailies have started being run in the slightly larger but much easier to read format. While most cartoonists had long complained about the poor treatment their strips had been receiving for years, Trudeau was the first to get his syndicate to agree to make it part of the conditions for carrying a strip. Due to the reluctance of editors to accept change, even when it's for an improvement, only a strip as popular as *Doonesbury* could have made such a demand and survived the backlash it created.

Editors accepted the demand largely because they wanted the strip, not because most believed the demand had any merit. The change Trudeau instituted has stuck and, thankfully, expanded to embrace other strips that editors decided on their own could benefit from the larger size.

Although Trudeau started out writing, pencilling, inking and even lettering the strip (and the lettering in the early strips leaves something to be desired), these days Trudeau just writes and pencils *Doonesbury* . He sends a Fax of the detailed penciled strip to his inker, Don Carlton, who lives near the home office of the Universal Press Syndicate in Kansas City.

The art on *Doonesbury* started out crude and gradually improved, but seldom rose above being functional and straightforward. Many panels were very static with little changing from one panel to the next other than a character's facial expression within an unmoving setting. Changes of angle and point of view were not something explored within the strip. In the case of *Doonesbury* it was always the words, not the image, which conveyed the message.

In 1980, Trudeau apparently decided it was time for a change and recognized there was room for growth in his traditional and highly recognizable approach to drawing the strip. Thus with his controversial tour through "Reagan's Brain" in 1980, the art took on new meaning and dimension and often was as interesting as the words which impelled it. This stylistic experimentation has continued over the years, both before and after Trudeau's hiatus from *Doonesbury* .

This change was hinted at in 1978, when he did several episodes without dialogue showing a transition from one scene to another to show that Joanie Caucus and Rick Redfern (the man she would eventually marry) had slept together. Showing two unmarried people in the same bed, however tastefully done as it was, was yet another first for newspaper comic strips, where such things were ordinarily never discussed.

While Trudeau's humor has largely been at the expense of the right side of the political spectrum, he's gone after targets on the left as well. Journalists, a favorite target of conservatives, have also taken their share of political barbs for being su-

perficial and credulous. When Roland Hedley, a supposed reporter for *Time* magazine, visited the Walden commune in the Seventies, everyone there made fun of him and told outrageous stories, which the journalist ran in his article without ever bothering to check their validity.

While black characters in the strip have largely been portrayed in a positive light, Trudeau chose to have one that went very much against the grain. Clyde, a black

male chauvinist, was portrayed as being both hip and superficial, considering his purchase of a new Buick not as a luxury, but a necessity. The following is one of the exchanges with his girlfriend, Virginia, over the car.

VIRGINIA: You bought this monstrosity?! How much, Clyde?

CLYDE: Six grand. But that there's one classy Buick! Worth every penny!

VIRGINIA: For God's sake, Clyde-you barely make that much in a year!

CLYDE: Been savin' though! 'N the down payment Weren't much, sugar! 'Sides, that machine is essential! It's for them nights when you 'n me go steppin' out 'round town!

VIRGINIA: Just what we needed-a $6,000 car to drive to Burger King in.

Trudeau is sensitive to the differences in going after targets who are rich, well-born and able and those at the bottom of the economic ladder. "I'm around underfoot, kicking in the shins, not the head," Trudeau stated in the Oct. 15, 1990 *Time* interview. It's clearly an issue he has decidedly un-liberal thoughts about. "At a seminar I heard Spike Lee tell

The art on Doonesbury started out crude and gradually improved, but seldom rose above being functional and straightforward. Many panels were very static with little changing from one panel to the next other than a character's facial expression within an unmoving setting. Changes of angle and point of view were not something explored within the strip. In the case of Doonesbury it was always the words, not the image, which conveyed the message.

whites they should be wondering to themselves why they were frightened when they see a group of young black men walking down the street. I was thinking, Spike, if you were walking down the street in $150 Nikes, you'd be calculating your chances, wondering, Will they recognize I'm Spike Lee?"

Like any political satirist, Trudeau's sharpest barbs are aimed at those occupying the positions of power in Washington. Apparently due to his on-going series about soldiers stationed in the Persian Gulf, Trudeau was bumped from the list of those going to visit the troops at Christmas in 1990. Although a spokesman for the White House claimed it was merely because of having too many names on the list of those scheduled to go, the satirist has indicated that he'll be surprised if he is rescheduled for a later visit as promised. Even before this incident, it was reported that the two political commentators Bush dislikes the most are Garry Trudeau and George Will—oddly enough from opposite sides of the political spectrum.

As part of his series of strips dealing with American troops in the Persian Gulf, his Dec. 9, 1990 installment touched a nerve when he reported on the little mentioned resentment soldiers and airmen have for sailors since Navy ships are all air conditioned, thus drastically reducing that aspect of the hardship for sailors stationed on ships in the Middle East. In San Diego, a Navy town, this strip did not go down well and *The San Diego Union* of Dec. 17, 1990, carried a column by William G. Stothers taking Trudeau to task for taking "a cheap shot" at sailors without explaining that ships have to be air conditioned in order to function.

Somehow I doubt that explanation, however legitimate, is any comfort to the soldiers and airmen stationed in the Saudi desert—Trudeau's entire point. Elsewhere in the same paper on the same day, Trudeau made news again when he appeared at his alma mater, Yale, for a signing of his latest collection, *Recycled Doonesbury* . Yale, as mentioned, is where the strip originated under the title *Bull Tales* .

Regarding his series on the Persian Gulf, Trudeau says it has been accepted by readers, even though he usually gets criticism if his strip gets stuck on one angle for a prolonged period. "Normally I'd get some mail," Trudeau said, but not in this case. "It's an indication of just how much this is on everybody's minds. You turn on any talk radio show and it's all we've been hearing, especially near the holidays."

During the signing, Trudeau met several second-generation *Doonesbury* fans—readers who weren't even born when the strip began in 1970. When one of them said he learned everything he knows about Richard Nixon and Watergate from reading old *Doonesbury* strips, Trudeau suggested his version of history was by no means complete. "There may be a few holes here and there," the cartoonist said.

That Trudeau also has fans among the troops in the Persian Gulf was proven on Sunday, Jan. 27, 1991 when *Doonesbury* included some special guest 'toons submitted by an airman stationed at Central Command in Saudi Arabia, under the title *Living In Purgatory*. Using the pen name "Zorro," the mystery cartoonist used cartoons to relate his observations on morale problems of all kinds, including criticism of the Pentagon's no-rotation policy. Only one newspaper chose not to run the strip while others called to verify that the cartoons were indeed by an American serviceman.

Trudeau's syndicate explained that "Zorro" is an airman who wrote to Trudeau and the cartoonist responded, seeking permission to use the drawings. Jerry Ceppos, managing editor of the *San Jose Mercury-News*, said, "I think it's interesting that, because of the way the military is handling these things, we're learning more about life on the front from the cartoon than from the Pentagon."

There already was a much publicized case of a serviceman whose letters to the hometown newspaper where he used to work were being published, until the Pentagon insisted it "approve" them first. This was due to the reservist's comments on morale and what daily life was like for soldiers stationed in the Persian Gulf, far from home and family, and that was before the shooting started.

As *Doonesbury* heads towards the 20th anniversary of its appearance on the newspaper comic strip page, we can see that a lot has changed in that time . While Trudeau still deals with certain issues more sharply than others in his comic strip, others have followed his lead in opening up the range of their expression, albeit not with the same intensity of purpose. At least the comics page doesn't remain quite as isolated from real life in its satirical concerns as it once did, and that is solely because of the inroads made by Garry Trudeau and *Doonesbury* .

THE FAR SIDE

Gary Larson succeeded in one of the most difficult areas of comic strips: the single panel cartoon. Without the benefit of continuing characters, he took on the Herculean task of coming up with different, off-the-wall gags seven days a week and maintained an incredibly high level of creative inspiration. It was no wonder that eventually he had to take a year off. Today he has cut back to creating original cartoons, but only six days a week, and The Far Side appears in more than 700 newspapers.

All visuals this chapter ©1991 Universal Press Syndicate

by Dan Whitworth and James Van Hise

"The Sixties offered the easy aphoristic wisdom of Charles Schultz, the self-satisfied Seventies the prickly satire of Garry Trudeau. The Reagan Eighties have spawned the demonic, subtle and slightly despairing humor of a former music store clerk."

—-*Rolling Stone* magazine

"I could say that the work of Gary Larson is absolutely unique, and that it will make you laugh your butt off, and that is true, but it means nothing in itself because in the '80s there are at least two dozen cartoonists who can make you laugh your butt off, and all of them are unique. We are living in the Golden Age of print cartoons, friends and neighbors, and the Q.E.D. of the postulate is that we simply take them for granted: Jim (*Garfield*) Davis, Charles (*Charlie*) Rodriguez, Charles (*Peanuts*) Schultz, Garry (*Doonesbury*) Trudeau, Berke (*Bloom County*) Breathed. . . and those are just for starters. Gary Larson, however, is *uniquely* unique.

—-Stephen King, from the foreword to *The Far Side Gallery 2*

"I Once the normal child of a car salesman and a secretary, Gary Larson has certainly seen some changes and now occupies a unique niche in the history of the comics: he is the first, and so far only, nationally syndicated cartoonist to achieve great success *and* have a newly discovered insect species named after him. *Strigiphilus garylarsoni,* a chewing tick found only on a certain genus of owls, is a fitting tribute to the strange workings of Larson's mind and pen. His cartoons have not simply engaged (and sometimes confounded) the imagination of the general public; they also have inspired a loyal following among the scientific community as well.

This, of course, is a direct result of Larson's own fascination with biology. As a child, he collected lizards and frogs, and even went so far as to create a full-blown swamp in his back yard. Later in life, he had a close call with a Burmese python he had raised from a baby, but survived to pursue a career in cartooning.

"Cartoon humor is strange," Larson explained in *The Pre-History of The Far Side* , "in that it's a totally silent world of creation and reaction. The cartoonist never hears laughter, groans, curses, fits of rage or anything. (Actually, maybe that's kind of nice.) It's a daily shoot-in-the-dark approach to humor; some things hit their target and some don't."

Oddly enough, he never gave much thought to becoming a cartoonist. It happened almost accidentally. Born in Tacoma, Wash. in 1950, he studied communications at Washington State University but without any specific career goals in mind. At the time his only real interest in cartoons came from being a fan of *Mad* magazine cartoonist Don Martin, but he never seriously considered pursuing that interest. His real first love was music. Some time after graduation, and fed up with his job at a music store (the closest his love of music had taken him to a professional career), Larson took a few days off to think about what he wanted to do with his life. Rather than concentrate on this burning question, he found himself at his kitchen table, drawing, and wound up producing six cartoons.

"Exactly why, I'll never know," Larson explained in his 1989 book *The Pre-History of The Far Side* . "Other than an interest in *Mad* magazine during my adolescence, and an appreciation for Gahan Wilson's work in *Playboy*, I knew nothing about the cartooning world. On the other hand, cartooning is not exactly a field that requires a graduate degree, complete with upper division courses like Noses 401 and Crossed Eyes 502."

The real reason dinosaurs became extinct

He describes the cartoons now as six of the worst that cartoondom had ever seen, but at the time his enthusiasm over the completed work knew no bounds. The next day he took the cartoons to a local Seattle magazine, *Pacific Search*, and received a check for $90. It seemed, suddenly, there was something to this cartooning business. Larson quit his job and developed a strip called *Nature's Way*, and sold it to a small weekly newspaper, the *Sumner News Review*. Unfortunately, $3 per cartoon was not enough money to support a career change, so he eventually gave it up and took a job as an investigator for the Humane Society. He never told them that he ran over a dog on the way to the interview.

In 1979, someone showed Larson's work to an editor at the *Seattle Times*, and *Nature's Way* was revived as a weekly feature. Although Larson's drawing style was not as smooth and simplified as it later became, the cartoons were concerned with the same basic obsessions as the later *Far Side*, and even included rough versions of later *Far Sides*.

Later that year, Larson took his portfolio to San Francisco during his vacation from the Humane Society and tried to see an editor at the *San Francisco Chronicle* in the hope of expanding his market. Without an appointment, without even knowing who to talk to, he bluffed his way as far as the cartoon editor's receptionist, who did little to encourage him but did take his portfolio. After two days of fruitless phone calls to learn whether the editor had reviewed his samples, Larson decided to retrieve his portfolio and head home, only to find that the editor had seen his cartoons and liked them. His trip had been a success: the *Chronicle* would run his work.

On his return home, however, he found a letter informing him that the *Seattle Times* was dropping *Nature's Way*. The cartoon, perhaps poorly placed next to a children's puzzle feature, had been drawing too many complaints. The following day Larson learned that his panel, to be renamed *The Far Side* , was to be syndicated as well. His success was assured.

"On Jan. 1, 1980, a single-panel cartoon called *The Far Side* debuted in the *San Francisco Chronicle* , and several months later, Chronicle Features began officially offering it to other newspapers," Larson recalled. "My first month in syndication, I *Mad* e about $100. I thought it would be exciting if I ever got up to the level where I could pay my rent. Two years later, Andrews and McMeel, the publishing arm of another syndicate—Universal—brought out my first book, also called *The Far Side* .

Testing whether or not animals "kiss"

Very much to my own surprise, and the collective shock of decent *Garfield*-loving people everywhere, it became a successful publication. It seemed natural, then, when my first contract expired in 1984, to move to Andrews and McMeel's parent company, Universal Press Syndicate." By 1985, Larson's income from *The Far Side* was reported well into six figures annually.

Of course, just as it had during its short run in the *Seattle Times*, controversy was certain to follow. In 1982, the "Cow Tools" panel provoked an outburst of public confusion. For some reason, no one seemed to get the joke, and the letters started pouring in.

"But, for the first time, Cow Tools awakened me to the fact that my profession was not just an isolated exercise in the corner of my apartment," Larson explained. The cow tools were just supposed to be meaningless artifacts. It was just a funny idea, that's all, but not everyone believed the answer was that simple.

"The day after its release, my phone began to ring with inquiries from reporters and radio stations from regions in the country where *The Far Side* was published. Everyone, it seemed, wanted to know what in the world this cartoon *meant!* My syndicate was equally bombarded, and I ultimately was asked to write a press release explaining Cow Tools. Someone sent me the front page of one newspaper which, down in one corner, ran the tease, *Cow Tools: What does it mean? (See pg. B14)* I was mortified."

On the other hand, he doesn't think it's necessary for people to understand everything he draws. "If I didn't understand a cartoon in a newspaper, I'd just turn the page. When people don't get the strip, I like that. I like th*The Far Side* can be confusing, because that means I'm still being experimental. People try to look for deep meanings in my work. I want to say, 'They're just cartoons, folks. You laugh or you don't.' Gee, I sound shallow. But I don't react to current events or other stimuli. I don't read or watch TV to get ideas. My work is basically sitting down at the drawing table and getting silly."

Other responses were a bit more negative, however, than people just complaining that they were confused. Sometimes people feel they understand a cartoon all too well. Some traditional forms of cartoon violence, such as the enmity between cats and dogs, didn't seem to sit too well with certain members of the populace. The "Tethercat" panel of 1988, depicting two dogs playing tetherball with a cat tied to a pole, provoked one angry reader to suggest that Larson be fined $1,000 for the cartoon, and for any others like it.

Tempers flare when Professors Carlson and Lazzell, working independently, ironically set their time machines to identical coordinates.

More ire was aroused by a cartoon showing a cat tied up and hanging outside a window; the angry readers failed to realize that the culprit here was the family dog, but interpreted the panel as indicating that the cat had been set out *for* the dog by the cat's owners. One reader even equated Larson with people who use small animals to train fighting dogs. Larson was amused, at least, by the fact that they misread his intentions entirely.

"I've honestly never set out to deliberately offend anyone (well, maybe that one time)," the cartoonist stated. "All I've really done, like most cartoonists, is just followed my own intuition and sensibilities of what's funny and what isn't. I think there's nothing else a cartoonist, stand-up comic, writer, or whoever *can* do. I mean, it's not that I necessarily wouldn't draw a cartoon like *Henry* or *Snuffy Smith* or *Blondie*; it's that I *can't*. If I drew *Blondie*, for example, it would still come out looking like *The Far Side* ; Daisy would get rabies and bite Dagwood, who'd go insane and have Mr. Dithers stuffed—whatever that means."

Another strip, in which a female ape accuses her husband of "conducting . . . research with that Jane Goodall tramp," provoked an outraged letter from the Jane Goodall Institute. When the *National Geographic* requested permission to reprint the cartoon, Larson's editor explained the situation, and withheld permission. The *Geographic* looked into the matter and discovered that Goodall herself liked the cartoon, and had no awareness of the controversy. Apparently, someone on her staff had taken it upon themselves to defend Goodall's honor against this heinous cartoonist.

Eventually, the cartoon was reprinted, and Larson eventually met Goodall at her research center in Africa. This, and the honor of having a new tick named after him, demonstrates the positive response that scientists have shown towards Larson's work. Of course, the simple fact that scientists appear so often in his work may also be related to this phenomenon. Cows, of course, occur even more frequently, but their opinion of *The Far Side* has yet to be *Mad* e known.

While the single panel cartoon had been around in newspapers for decades, prior to *The Far Side* the humor had remained pretty traditional. Weird humor, the truly offbeat and black humor, had been reserved for other publications, not the daily newspaper. The cartoons of Charles Addams ran in slick magazines, as did the even more strange cartoons of Gahan Wilson. While Wilson did break into the newspaper Sunday comics page in the Seventies, the cartoons there were toned down from the kind of work you'd find him doing in *Playboy*, *Fantasy & Science Fiction* and other traditionally adult markets.

Sixty-five million years ago, when cows ruled the earth

When Gary Larson started doing the kind of cartoons that the guys in the office loved, it was inevitable that new ground would be broken as to what people at home would think of it. Cartoons with alligators and sharks, which always played off the predatory nature of the beasts, tended to disturb people. One startling cartoon showed what looked to be sharks attacking people from a sinking ship, but the caption and a closer examination revealed that the bodies were simply mannikins, and the sharks reacted to the situation as though it were a cruel hoax.

Alligators were shown in one cartoon to be leaping after monkeys hanging above the water (the tail wrapped around a branch was all that remained of one monkey), while another showed 'gators crowded around a tub whose contents were obscured, although what they were doing was revealed by the caption, "Bobbing For Poodles." Not everyone was ready for this. As explained above, even a cartoon as simple and offbeat as "Cow Tools" stirred people up because they believed they were missing some deeper meaning obscured by the surface images. *The Far Side* definitely knew how to touch a nerve, even among people who didn't understand what they were reacting to.

The humor of the absurd is often the cutting edge Gary Larson uses to shape his ideas. Cows and snakes are often subjects of his gags, but in ways nature never intended. Now while talking cows and anthropomorphic snakes are nothing new on the comics page, a vampire cow and a snake curled around a huge food dish which has the name "Garfield" on it are distinctly in the realm of the unusual. Even Sunday was not spared its startling images in Larson's strip, as the one labeled "Young Jimmy Frankenstein" ably demonstrates. The sight of a little boy and a patchwork dog (with one duck's foot) might tend to look odd in juxtaposition with *Hi & Lois* and *The Wizard Of Id*."

While not all Larson's cartoons are this demented or disturbing, they all have an undercurrent of thinking about things in unusual ways. This leads to that question that all people who have a creative bent (and some are more bent than others), are inevitably confronted with: "Where do you get your ideas?" In Larson's case, he's also asked "*Why* do you get your ideas?" The two are somewhat related, though. In dealing with the first question, Larson said, "I've always found the question interesting, because it seems to embody a belief that there exists some secret, tangible place of origin for cartoon ideas.

"Every time I hear it, I'm struck by this mental image where I see myself rummaging through my grandparents' attic and coming across some old, musty trunk. Inside I find this equally old and elegant-looking book. I take it in my hands, blow away the dust, and embossed on the front cover in large, gold script is the title, *Five Thousand and One Weird Cartoon Ideas*.

"I'm afraid the real answer is much more mundane: I don't know where my ideas come from. I will admit, however, that one key ingredient is caffeine. I get a couple cups of coffee into me and weird things just start to happen."

Regular, or even irregular readers, of *The Far Side* can certainly attest to that! And yet Larson doesn't consider his cartoon to be as bizarre as many of his readers do. "I've never found the cartoon itself bizarre. I think *Nancy* is bizarre. I don't deny people the right to think it, but I look at *The Love Boat*, and it has a laugh track, so evidently it's something that most people find funny. But I find *The Love Boat* bizarre."

Writing *The Far Side* doesn't always come easy for Larson, though. "Sometimes you're on a roll," he explained, "but other times I just sit there and sweat. I think I'm maintaining the quality, but internally I'm paying for it."

In a 1977 interview, his concern about maintaining the level of quality and creativity was apparent when he said, "I think the strip is riding a wave, and I don't know when it's going to crest. Things are very cyclical in this society. I worry about doing it for another 20 years. I think it would just be nice to be remembered. . . to no longer be a cartoonist. . . to quit soon enough so that people would say, 'Hey, remember *The Far Side*? That was a funny cartoon.' I mean, there are other things to do in life. Like play the guitar."

In fact, Larson himself admitted at one point to being "burned-out," and in late 1988 he announced that he was taking a 14-month hiatus from *The Far Side*. He became only the second cartoonist (Garry Trudeau did so a few years earlier) to take such an extended vacation from a strip only to later return revitalized.

"All I want to do is purge cartooning from my mind," Larson told *Forbes* magazine In December 1988. In his time off he relaxed by playing jazz guitar and jotting down cartoon ideas for his planned return. The hiatus began Oct. 30, 1988, but return he did, on schedule. His renewed creativity was readily apparent. That Larson took the need for a vacation seriously is evidenced by the fact that *The Far Side* was appearing in 825 papers at the time he took his leave of absence. Reruns of early strips ran during his vacation, many which had been seen in only a few papers since *The Far Side* only had 40 client papers when it began. Few papers chose not to carry the reruns.

Larson was experiencing other pressures related to the strip when, in a 1985 interview, he complained about the pressures of celebrity. These included fans recognizing him and taking pictures of his house, which he tried to head off by ceasing public appearances around his home base of Seattle.

Down at the Eat and Slither

"It used to be simple," he explained. "Draw the panels and send them out. Now it's too show biz. I'm going to pull the plug, when necessary, to keep my sanity." On the other hand he also expressed a healthy skepticism about his lifestyle and career when he said, "I can't imagine drawing cartoons in a Third World country. I keep

THE FAR SIDE By Gary Larson

© 1990 Universal Press Syndicate

"Barbara, you just have to come over and see all my eggs. The address is: Doris Griswold, 5 feet 4 inches, 160 pounds, brown eyes — I'm in her hair."

THE FAR SIDE By Gary Larson

© 1991 Universal Press Syndicate

SCORPION PETTING ZOO

FARM ANIMALS

Innovative concepts in exposing city kids to nature

thinking someone's gonna' show up and say, 'There's been a big mistake. The guy next door is supposed to be drawing the cartoon. Here's your shovel.' "

Another fallout of success was the fact that a Seattle area bar named itself *The Far Side* Tavern, but he chose to just shrug off the swipe of his strip's name with the observation, "I wish them well, whoever they are. At least they have good taste. At least it's not called the Garfield Bar and Grill."

As mentioned earlier, not everyone enjoys or appreciates *The Far Side* . The editor of the Fort Wayne Indiana *News-Sentinel* tried to drop the strip because, "It too frequently played to the humor of violence." Readers protested and the strip's place on the comics page was preserved. To complaints such as this, Larson responds, "Morbid humor is very valid, even healthy, as long as you don't do it gratuitously. There's more violence in Saturday morning cartoons."

One of the most incisive comments on Larson's strip appeared in the Oct. 5, 1990 issue of *Entertainment Weekly*. Writing there, Ken Tucker observed: "These are the most consistently witty non sequiturs, puns and common sense observations being created in America, in any medium. Gary Larson has brought laugh-out-loud humor back to the funny pages with one-panel drawings that combine surrealism with an amateur's interest in science to create a comic tone that's at once eccentric and aggressive. A snake on the witness stand in a courtroom hisses at a prosecuting attorney, 'Of *course* I did it in cold blood, you idiot! I'm a reptile.' When *The Far Side* started in the late '70s, some readers were shocked by its more macabre panels, but in these Andrew Dice Clay days Larson's drawings seem downright elegant in the precision of their black humor."

And besides that, it's just wonderfully bizarre.

"Okay, here we go again . . . one . . . two . . ."

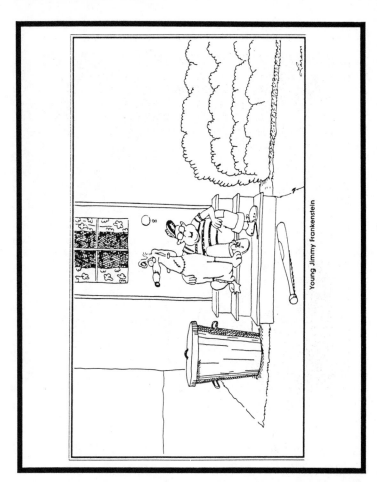

Young Jimmy Frankenstein

"What is this? . . . Some kind of cruel hoax?"

"The revolution has been postponed . . . We've discovered a leak."

GARFIELD

Often cited by other cartoonists as a symbol of the decline of comic strip creativity due to its overwhelming popularity and merchandising magic, the strip remains tirelessly alive with good natured slapstick humor and characters who draw you back day after day. Started by Jim Davis in 1978, the strip is now largely the work of talented assistants, who keep the fat cat very active indeed.

by James Van Hise

Cartoonists tend to couch their comments about *Garfield* in diplomatic terms. What they don't deny is the strip's incredible popularity. In 1983, Berke Breathed was asked how his own strip, *Bloom County*, stacked up against *Garfield* . He remarked, "Well, nothing stacks up to *Garfield* , which is one of the most widely-distributed strips in history, so we all kind of pale in comparison to that. *Garfield* is carried in about 1,000 papers, so we're doing pretty good at 400."

A very good indication of the *Garfield* phenomenon is that a strip as popular as *Bloom County* was in 1983 was in less than half as many papers as *Garfield*. Probably no other strip even comes close to the success of *Garfield*, with the possible exception of the venerable *Peanuts* or *Blondie*, and it shows no signs of wear and tear. Seven years later the strip's popularity has spread worldwide and *Garfield* appears in 2,000 newspapers in 7 languages and 22 countries. Its success goes on and on.

More than 30 books reprint his comic strip antics in both color and black and white and major bookstores often stock as many of the different volumes as possible. That's not unusual since at one point, 7 of the reprint books were on the *New York Times* best-seller list at the same time. Never mind that comic strip reprints are listed on the "non-fiction" best-seller list (that's another issue altogether). If some people bemoan how many licensed items *Garfield* graces, that may be because at one point the funny feline had his likeness attached to some 3,000 products. No wonder newspaper syndicates want to try to imitate *Garfield* 's amazing success.

Jim Davis, the writer/artist who created *Garfield* , didn't start out to be a cartoonist. "I thought about being a doctor, a scientist and a teacher," Davis told *National Geographic World* in 1985. "I was shy, and drawing became my way of expressing myself. I learned that I could make people laugh with my drawings."

He started drawing as a child because he often found himself bedridden from asthma, which he'd been stricken with as a baby and which almost killed him when he was 9. "You have to do something when you're lying in bed, so you play with your mind." It was his mother who helped Davis find his interest in drawing.

"She's the one who got me started. She'd give me a paper and pencil and make me try to draw. I'd draw someone, and as soon as I learned to spell, I'd have them saying something. Then I started drawing boxes and in second or third grade, it was cartooning."

Davis grew up in Indiana on a farm which seldom had fewer than 25 cats roaming the property—insuring that his observations about feline behavior are not entirely drawn from his imagination. "There were always cats there," Davis said. "They were a lot stronger and hardier than *Garfield* could ever be, but they were my playmates. There's not much else to do on a farm; we didn't go bowling a lot." His restless interest in drawing drew much of its youthful inspiration from these ever-present felines.

At Fairmont High School (also the alma mater of James Dean), Davis drew a little cartoon he called *Herman*. Later, at Ball State University, Davis studied business and claims to have earned one of the lowest grade point averages in the history of the university. As a result, he dropped out of college and managed to land a job as a pasteup boy in the Art Department at a Muncie, Ind. advertising agency for the munificent wage of $1.60 an hour. In 1969 he was married to Carolyn Alterkruse, and two months later secured the job of assistant to artist Tom Ryan on the comic strip *Tumbleweeds*.

"I always loved the cartoons," Davis admits, "but I never seriously thought I could do it for a living until I started with Tom." From Tom Ryan, Davis learned the genuine discipline needed to draw as well as the techniques for maintaining a strip.

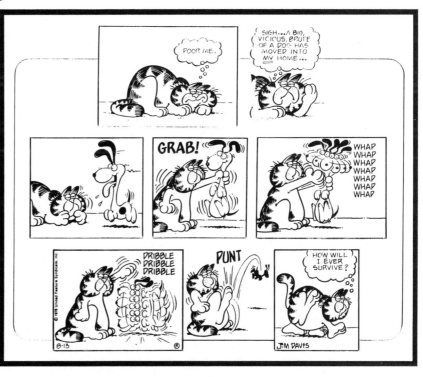

"I learned from Tom what it takes to maintain a syndicated feature. He paid a lot of attention to his writing. There weren't many surprises when I started *Garfield*. For years I watched Tom handle the fan mail, interviews and things of that nature. Also, working with him afforded me the time, income and confidence to keep pursuing syndication myself. As I watched him do a successful strip I thought, 'I can do that too.' "

Davis then drew up his own idea for a comic strip, *Gnorm the Gnat*, but it was a difficult endeavor. "One of the toughest things was the motivation. It's hard to keep interested enough to keep drawing and drawing and drawing when you have no guarantee anything will come of it. Sure, it's fun to be whimsical; just to sit there and doodle, but to really think a character through is tough." After five years of rejections, Davis accepted the fact that perhaps bugs weren't what the newspaper comic strip syndicates were looking for.

He then decided to create a completely different strip, one which didn't feature insects. "I took a long, hard look at the comics," he recalled. "I saw there were a lot

of dogs doing very well—Snoopy, Marmaduke. . . " But he didn't notice any cats. "When I thought about using a cat it became simply a mental exercise: What would happen if I crossed a primal animal such as a cat with a human being? What would I get?

"The answer was that I'd get a very selfish animal, someone out for his own creature comforts; somebody very egotistical, yet so honest people can't dislike him. This gave me a lot of latitude with the humor. Since people naturally attribute human feelings and thoughts to cats, I could write for him as an animal or as a human. Anyway I pleased, really. In fact, the more human I've made Garfield the more catlike people say he is."

Even after creating the strip, he continued working for Ryan while he developed and reworked the idea for the strip. Originally the main character was Jon Arbuckle, who happened to own this cat named Garfield. By refocusing the gags and bringing the cat into the spotlight, it started coming together because, as he put it, "the cat had all the punch lines."

When he started trying to sell it, he met with only two rejections before Davis made a deal with United Feature Syndicate in January 1978. What's so incredible about this is that each cartoon syndicate sees an average of 1,500 comic strip ideas a year, from which they ultimately pick one or two, and of the new strips the syndicates attempt to market each year, the chances are that only one in 50 will succeed.

"Carolyn never doubted I would get syndicated," Davis says of his wife's confidence in him. "She provided a great home life and a lot of support. It was blind faith on her part. Quite frankly, at 32, I was getting a little nervous. After nine years of rejection slips it occurs to you that you may never be syndicated. When the news finally came it was like retiring. I no longer had to work for a living. I'd be doing what I liked best to do."

Garfield made his grand entrance in the newspapers of America June 19, 1978. Well, not in all the newspapers in America. In 41 of the newspapers in America, but it was a breakthrough nonetheless and Davis celebrated in high fashion by buying a newer model used car than his old used car was. Two years later he had a best-selling collection of *Garfield* flying off the shelves in bookstores and his client papers had increased to a respectable 200.

In fact the strip had already developed such a loyal following that when newspapers in Chicago, Little Rock and Salt Lake City attempted to drop the strip from their comics pages, vast numbers of irate fans forced them to bring it back. Early in 1980 the strip was picking up about six newspapers a month, but a representative of the United Feature Syndicate said that after the first *Garfield* book came out and hit the best-seller list, "we've added papers at the rate of about 30 a month."

"The answer was that I'd get a very selfish animal, someone out for his own creature comforts; somebody very egotistical, yet so honest people can't dislike him. This gave me a lot of latitude with the humor. Since people naturally attribute human feelings and thoughts to cats, I could write for him as an animal or as a human. Anyway I pleased, really. In fact, the more human I've made Garfield the more cat-like people say he is."

In light of the success of the book, United Features arranged a media blitz and Davis hit the talk show circuit. Today, *Garfield* is in 2,000 papers worldwide and the strip speaks for itself without any need for special promotions on the part of its creator. After all, as Davis so aptly put it, "*Garfield* is famous. I am not."

In describing Garfield, Davis states, "He's a little bit of Archie Bunker and Morris the Cat tossed together. He's a very calculating cat. He's a very believable cat." The cartoonist named his comic strip cat after his grandfather, who died when Davis was only 5. Recalling his grandfather, Davis said, "He had a huge lap. I remember looking up his nostrils most of the time. He was a huge man; a very stubborn man. A very opinionated man and cantankerous."

Today, in spite of the mammoth success of *Garfield* , Davis still lives and works in Indiana. "Everything I did cannot erase the fact that I am an Indiana farm boy. Except for the media attention, precious little has changed." To handle the increasing demands of the strip and its licensing offshoots, Davis established a studio in Muncie in 1981. Called PAWS, he works there along with his assistants. From the studio he both works on the strip and oversees all licensing.

"We design Garfields for each and every product. The thought of rubber-stamping them isn't for me. I have a real conscience about licensing," Davis stated. The staff at PAWS, Inc. grew quickly, and by 1984 it numbered two dozen. "Artists are rumored to be temperamental. We're supposed to have big flare-ups and personality conflicts, but we don't. We've only had two turnover since we started. Must be the country air," Davis observed in a 1984 interview in *The Saturday Evening Post*. The home Davis shares with his family is just down a path from the country studio.

When the strip began in 1978, Garfield looked somewhat different than the character does today. Although the cat was modified over the course of the first year into the form we're familiar with now, originally Garfiel was even fatter than the present form, and he looked like an older cat rather than like a young mischievous one. In some respects, he looked more like a real cat than like an idealized cartoon kitty. Davis explained the changes by saying that not only did Garfield grow stripes, but, "His eyes got larger to get more expression; so did his mouth. His body got a little smaller just so I could get him around easier. His limbs got longer to make him more animated and his ears got a little shorter because I didn't need them."

In his foreword to the book *Great Comic Cats* (1981), Jim Davis discussed his love for felines and how it combined with his love of comics to produce *Garfield* .

"Al Capp once told me it takes two things to be a cartoonist: first, it helps to have been dropped on your head as a small child; second, you must have no desire, talent or ability to do anything useful in life. There's a certain amount of truth to that," Davis observed. "At times I feel a bit silly drawing funny pictures of kitty cats for a living. Perhaps I shouldn't feel that way; after all, there are even sillier people paying me to do it.

"Admittedly, cartooning is my first love, and, obviously, cats are another love of mine. But, when I decided to combine the two a few years ago, I was in no way prepared for the reception *Garfield* would be given. Cat lovers are the most zealous of all the pet lovers in the world!

"People naturally attribute human traits and qualities to cats because cats are so laid back. Not only does one feel that a cat thinks in English, but that it also has the ability to read what is on one's mind. Quite frankly, I treat Garfield as a human in a cat suit. Of all domesticated animals, cats have more of their primal instincts intact. Combining a human personality with a primal animal is intriguing but not all that challenging. Way down deep we are all motivated by the same urges that motivate cats. Cats have the courage to live by them.

"While cats are very independent, they seem to demand the devotion of their owners. I have had the opportunity to visit with literally thousands of cat lovers. Sometimes it is hard to tell where the owner leaves off and the cat starts. One best-selling author confided his cat helps him write his novels. Every moment spent at the typewriter involves his cat either sitting on his lap or lying on his shoulder sharing his consciousness and contributing cat energy to the creative flow. Call it anything you like but that cat has helped make his owner a millionaire and quite famous to boot.

Davis continued, "The late James Dean was from my hometown of Fairmont, Ind. He privately attributed much of his acting method to the study of cats. As a youth he would mimic the resting, yawning and stretching gestures of his farm cats as a relaxation exercise before his stage appearances. He admired cats for the nervous energy they contained under a thin veneer of passive grace.

"A senior executive of a prominent publishing company told of his cat's passion for his wife's piano playing. For 14 years the cat would curl up atop the piano as Sarah played and never moved 'til she was through. One night, quite elderly and quite ill, the cat crawled onto the keyboard of the piano, buried its face in its paws, and quietly passed away . . . a testament to its love for her music. I don't know how many times he told that story, but tears still welled up in his eyes as he finished it.

"Cats are perfect for comics," Davis observed. "They are at once subtle, physical, thoughtful and slapstick. They have tremendous latitude. Since they aren't obviously of a particular sex, age or race, they can move into many areas and make comments on many subjects that are restricted for their human counterparts. A cat pummeling a dog is quite natural . . . a man pummeling a dog is considered bad form. Several of Garfield 's personal traits, such as overeating, oversleeping, and not exercising are endearing in cats and disgusting in humans.

"Cats are universally loved, hated, feared and worshipped. Where better to anthropomorphize our furry brothers and sisters than in the comics?" Davis added.

Needless to say, cats have been popularized in cartoons and comic strips for many years even before *Garfield* joined the clan. In cartoons there were cats in such series as *Tom and Jerry, Pixie and Dixie, Felix the Cat* as well as *Tweety and Sylvester*. Comics strips, of course, include the classic *Crazy Kat, Nard n' Pat, Heathcliff, Gordo* (with Gato, which is Spanish for cat, along with an adult black cat named

P.M. and a kitten, Bete Noire). And who can forget Robert Crumb's Fritz the Cat, the first cat to star in an X-rated animated motion picture, albeit one which bore little resemblance to the material from which it drew its inspiration. Underground comics also presented Fat Freddy's Cat, a more realistic, if satirical, portrayal of your average house cat. Then, of course, there's also Garfield.

Garfield seems to appeal to all ages but clearly has a legion of supporters among children, as evidenced by the popularity of the animated cartoons made for television wherein the voice of Garfield (we hear him thinking although he doesn't actually talk) is rendered by the inimitable Lorenzo Music.

When we first met the overweight, always hungry Garfield , he was sharing quarters with his owner, Jon Arbuckle (whom creator Jim Davis patterned somewhat after himself), and Jon's roommate, Lyman. But while Lyman's drooling dog, Odie, still bounds around on the scene, Lyman has done a fadeout. For a time a kitten named "Nermal" was added to the strip to act as Garfield's nemesis because, "He's always had this thing against cute," Davis stated, talking about Garfield's personal outlook on life. "He says, 'Cute rots the intellect.' " But the action in recent years has been streamlined to include Garfield, Odie and Jon almost exclusively.

While Garfield is portrayed as being lazy, voracious and shameless, Odie is almost the exact opposite, except that the dog is basically portrayed as being too blissfully stupid to have anything approaching a personality. No matter what torments, teasing and dirty tricks Garfield pulls on Odie, the dog always springs back good-naturedly for more, seemingly unruffled by Garfield's parade of tortures.

A less than enthusiastic appraisal of *Garfield* appeared in a feature article, *Black & White & Read All Over* in the Oct. 5, 1990 issue of *Entertainment Weekly*. Writer Ken Tucker observed, "Like *Peanuts*, *Garfield* is now more a marketing phenomenon than a comic strip. There is something likable about this sarcastic cat, and when the cat's creator, Jim Davis, is indulging his mean streak, *Garfield* features the most sadistic visual slapstick this side of a classic Road Runner cartoon. But too often the art is just perfunctory, the jokes lame."

But it works.

Garfield has managed to make weird, and at times violent, humor palatable. One of Odie the dog's more pronounced characteristics is his tendency to drool, and drool and drool. Puddles of drool sometimes appear in the strip, but because it's a dog we accept it. If the strip did jokes about people leaving puddles of drool, readers would turn the pages so quickly the newspaper would get torn in half. Violence appears in the form of *Garfield* and Odie roughing each other up, but while *Garfield* may attack Jon and shred his clothes, Jon does not respond in kind. Thus the violence stays within proscribed lines.

Slapstick emerges from time to time, often in the form of gags about food, and even food fights. I guess because it's the kind of war Garfield wouldn't mind fighting in on a regular basis.

Speaking of food, fat jokes are a mainstay in the strip. Mostly they center around Garfield eating everything in sight, but occasionally the cat's attempts to celebrate being fat are just an excuse to poke fun at same. In 1979 an entire seven-day span was dubbed by Garfield as "National Fat Week."

Garfield : "Out of the closet, you fatties! This week we're going to eat without guilt."

While Garfield is portrayed as being lazy, voracious and shameless, Odie is almost the exact opposite, except that the dog is basically portrayed as being too blissfully stupid to have anything approaching a personality.

Another day of that week dealt with a weight-height chart. According to that chart, if you weighed 200 pounds you should be 6',4". But Garfield observed, "That means if you're under 6'4" you're not overweight, you're undertall." Most of the gags, uttered by the fat cat, poked fun at being fat, an unlikely thing for a fat person to do. The token skinny joke was the following.

Garfield : "How many skinny people does it take to fill a shower? I don't know. They keep slipping down the drain.

Not quite as hard-hitting as the fat jokes. Thereafter the fat jokes only continued at Garfield's expense, but primarily he was shown enjoying being a glutton. "Actually, he relives a lot of guilt," Davis explained. "With the health craze and self-improvement kick going on, we're made to feel guilty for overeating, oversleeping and not exercising. Garfield helps balance the scales." Interestingly, when the strip began in 1978 Garfield was drawn as being even fatter than he is now. One memorable strip from July 2, 1978 showed Garfield deciding to jog, and after great effort he made it the few feet to his food dish. Considering how huge the cat was drawn as being, that was a believable ordeal.

In describing the humor in *Garfield* , Davis said it's not the topical humor of *Doonesbury* or the sophisticated humor of *Peanuts*. Rather he feels that it's "the kind of laugh that leaves you feeling a little better. A lot of hopeful cartoonists take the work too seriously. The more fun you have with it, the more fun people have reading it." Davis said the rule for a good cartoon is, "The fewer the words, the better the timing. Ta Da Ta Da Boom! Drawing a strip is like telling a joke. It *is* telling a joke."

He suggests that struggling cartoonists should, "draw and write as much as you can," but that uppermost, one should enjoy what they're doing. "If you have fun doing them, people will have fun reading them."

LIFE IN HELL

Although this strip began appearing in just a handful of weekly newspapers a decade ago, it has gained new life and new readers thanks to successful reprints now easily found in major bookstores around the country. The weekly strip continues today, its humor and satire undiminished by its creator's busy schedule since he launched The Simpsons.

by James Van Hise

"All my life I've been torn between frivolity and despair, between the desire to amuse and the desire to annoy, between dread-filled insomnia and a sense of my own goofiness. Just like you, I worry about love and sex and work and suffering and injustice and death, but I also dig drawing bulgy-eyed rabbits with tragic overbites. "Hence *Life In Hell*, an ongoing series of self-help cartoons—the self being helped being me. I don't know how helpful these cartoons have been, but drawing them over the last 10 years has sure amused me. I hope the cartoons amuse you too, but if you're one of those people who finds my stuff annoying, that's OK. Luckily for me, being annoying is a blast, too."

Matt Groening's introduction to *The Big Book of Hell* (1990)

Life In Hell is that strip the guy who created *The Simpsons* did before he created *The Simpsons*. Fans of offbeat comics and those who appreciate satire which has a broken razor's edge, appreciated *Life In Hell* from the start. Being that I frequented the Los Angeles area a great deal beginning from 1979 on, I read the alternative newspapers and was immediately drawn to this strip. While some people are attracted to strips by their art, I doubt that anyone could honestly admit that about the functional style employed on *Life In Hell*.

"Many comics are overdrawn," Groening stated. "The ideas don't warrant the trouble the artist goes to. Mine are just the opposite. I don't define myself as a cartoonist primarily, but as a writer. The fact that I'm able to do this comic-book form every day amazes me—it's part of the joke. I'm more interested in ideas than in visuals. My goal in cartooning is to entertain and subvert."

The images succeed in conveying the ideas Matt Groening chooses to explore. In some respects the art looks like a comic strip drawn by a talented child, but the subjects it explores range from recalling childhood experiences common to most of us as well as dealing with the most basic questions of our existence, including the one everyone asks at one time or another, "Why bother?"

Says Groening, "The real world is 10 times more hellish than *Life In Hell*. I think my stuff is therapeutic. It gives a laugh while sharing misery."

Matt Groening, like all cartoonists, expressed a fledgling interest in drawing as a child. As with many other youngsters, his teachers and other adults did their level best to discourage him. Groening resisted and persevered in the face of seemingly hopeless odds. As a child growing up in Portland, Ore., he's described himself as the type who was always in trouble. While he enjoyed the town he grew up in, and readily admits to an otherwise comfortable upbringing in a pleasant middle-class neighborhood, that was only one part of his growing years.

"School, on the other hand, was quite different because it was so boring for me. I think any kid who is curious and inquisitive would find the average public school to be a bit on the slow side, and that was certainly the case for me. I spent most of my waking hours drawing surreptitiously while the teacher droned on and on about something. I couldn't remember what. I just *felt* intuitively from a very early age that there was no need for adults to make life so miserable for kids. It seemed unfair that the kids were punished in the ways that they were, and because of my (smart) mouth and my insolent attitudes I certainly got in trouble quite a bit," Groening recalls. His childhood punishments were the classics: principal's office, desk in the hall, standing in the corner and even having his mouth taped shut.

In an interview with the *Los Angeles Times*, the cartoonist said those experiences caused him to arrive at one inescapable conclusion: "You are what you are basically despite school. I think there's a lot of unnecessary misery in education. I certainly felt it. Just the idea of punishing a kid for drawing stacks of cartoons, of ripping them up and throwing them away. Some of the stuff was senseless and immature, but other stuff was really creative, and I was amazed that there was no differentiation between the good stuff and the bad stuff, or very little."

When Groening created *The Simpsons*, Bart became the child whose every action flies in the face of authority, both parental and educational. When a harmless Bart Simpson T-shirt bearing the slogan "Underachiever and proud of it" (a poke at the labels children have inflicted on them by teachers) appeared on the market, educators attacked the shirt and some schools banned children from wearing it to class.

Groening's response was that of a man who had once again locked horns with an old nemesis, but now in a position to strike back and be heard. "What bugs me about it is that it's the kind of petty, stupid exertion of authority by intellectual boneheads that kids encounter every day. The real tragedy is that it breaks the spirit of a lot of them. I was lucky. With me it just made me more set in my ways."

Matt grew up the middle child of five siblings. Two of his sisters are named Maggie and Lisa, his mother's name is Margaret and his father's name is Homer. His father started out as a fledgling cartoonist, but made so little money at it that he soon directed his talents elsewhere, becoming a film maker and advertising man.

Because of his own experiences, even though he encouraged his son's artistic interests, he told Matt there was no future in being a cartoonist. Matt's interest in drawing cartoons continued nonetheless.

In high school, Matt and his friends founded their own school political party called Teens For Decency. He ran for school president with the motto "If You're Against Decency, What Are You For?" and won. The only thing was, Groening considered his group as a running parody of his classmates' concepts of what was normal.

When he decided to continue his education, he applied to Harvard as well as nearby Evergreen State College. Harvard didn't recognize Matt's talents but Evergreen did. "Evergreen was heaven for talent," Groening explains. "Brilliant teachers really talking about what they were enthusiastic about, no limits on the cameras and tape recorders and media tools you could check out."

His artistic abilities were shaped in many ways at the school. Part of this came from his friendship with a fellow student, artist Lynda Barry, who drew wild cartoons and convinced Matt to draw only what he thought was funny rather than attempting to play to what he perceived to be an audience's expectations. He used this advice to good stead when he became editor of the campus newspaper, the *Cooper Point Journal*.

In addition to being editor, he drew satirical cartoons for the journal, taking Lynda Barry's advice and drawing what he thought was funny instead of what he thought his imaginary audience wanted to see. As a result, he stung people. His ascerbic, dead-on commentaries of reality which pepper his *Life In Hell* strip of the Eighties and Nineties, gave birth kicking and screaming in the Seventies, but the screams came from offended readers. Groening thought he was jousting with the establishment, but what his cartoons often actually did was to prick the cherished illusions of his peers.

While the conservative political right often is regarded as being stuffy and humorless, they've got nothing on the solemnly serious political left. Then again, no one reacts well when their pomposity is poked. One particular cartoon satirized communes, a seemingly harmless and abstract target today, but not in the Seventies. One hundred students signed a protest petition and sent it as a letter to the editor, and above the signatures the letter read: "Dear Mr. Groening: Communal struggles are not funny!"

Even today the letters to the editor pages of newspapers occasionally can be found to contain letters from people who fail to realize that political cartoons make their points through exaggeration. People who often may find an artist's cartoons amusing, bristle if the cartoonist challenges a concept they find near and dear. Not all of society's sacred cows have been slain by the slings and arrows of impious cartoonists, but those few remaining have taken their share of artistic barbs.

As editor of the paper, Matt Groening expected to be one with the student body, anticipating that the teachers and faculty would be the ones to find his humor intemperate. The opposite, as noted above, would often result. One of his college cartoons rendered a cereal box labeled "Evergreen Flakes" with a crew of Grateful Dead clones gathered around a bowl of "leisure cereal of the state of Washington." Their motto: "Achievement without effort." The faculty loved it. Students mumbled in dismay. Groening was finding that his contemporaries were by no means as open minded and as willing to accept that share of the burden of society's problems as he believed.

In 1977, with college completed, Groening took the great step into trying to see if the commercial world was ready for his gimlet eye. At 23, he came to Los Angeles to find work as a writer. L.A.'s a big town, he thought. There should be plenty of opportunities. There are if one is willing to starve for several years while working to make them happen, which Matt did.

"It was the most miserable time of my life. Heartbreak is light and lively compared to unemployment." About Los Angeles at the time, he said, "I really hated it. It was very hot, very smoggy and very ugly."

He lived in Hollywood (not the glamor strip people outside California imagine it to be) and worked at a variety of odd jobs. Groening describes the period by saying, "It was the most miserable time of my life. Heartbreak is light and lively compared to unemployment." About Los Angeles at the time, he said, "I really hated it. It was very hot, very smoggy and very ugly."

It was during this time that his eye for truth and his own circumstances combined to inspire him to create a comic strip he called *Life In Hell*. He reproduced the first strips in a comic book he cranked out on a photo-copy machine, gave them away to friends and sold others for $2 a copy at the "Licorice Pizza" record store on the Sunset Strip, where he worked at the time.

Believing from some of the feedback that it could have a bigger life than his own meager self-publishing efforts could give it. He even sold a couple of installments of it to the counter-culture magazine *Wet*. In the fall of 1978, when he began working for the then new *L.A. Weekly* as a paste-up artist, he showed some of the *Life In Hell* strips to the then editor, who didn't warm to Groening's unusual cartoon. "I never intended to be a cartoonist," Matt stated. "I never say anything as crude as my stuff that was getting published."

FUNNY
STUFF

When Groening showed the strips to the editor of the rival *L.A. Reader* in 1979, he was intrigued enough to offer Groening a writing job on an assignment about billboard painters on the Sunset Strip. The piece ran and Matt was hired shortly thereafter as circulation manager of the *L.A. Reader*. What this entailed was to deliver copies of the *Reader* (a free weekly paper) in his own 1962 Dodge Dart on a route which took him from Glendale to Malibu. For those unfamiliar with the area, this spans the entire greater Los Angeles metropolitan area.

The editor of the *Reader* found more to appreciate in Groening's ascerbic cartoonings than the *L.A. Weekly* editor did and on April 25, 1980, the *Reader* debuted *Life In Hell*. At the time, the strip starred Binky, a rabbit inspired by one of his former college roommates. "We both had romantic problems," Groening explained. "Mine were earnest and tragic, and his were hilarious."

At first Binky was obnoxious and seemed bent on attacking the reader, so the strip was not exactly embraced with open arms upon its humble debut. "It annoyed readers and it annoyed editors, so I decided that instead of being arrogant, Binky would be a victim. The second my characters began to be tortured and alienated, the popularity began. The more I tortured them, the more readers loved me."

Within three years, 20 similar papers were carrying the strip. In 1986, *Life In Hell* was so popular that the *L.A. Weekly* lured Groening to its fold and its larger circulation. College friend Lynda Barry left the *Reader* with Groening. She had started a strip of her own called *Ernie Pook's Comic*. It is just as quirky in its own unique way as Groening's is.

Life In Hell is largely about characters who look like rabbits, but whose world looks much like our own, and they even interact with human beings. There's Binky, an adult. Bongo, his illegitimate son, has one ear. Sheba is Bongo's rarely-seen estranged girlfriend. Others are Akbar and Jeff, two little guys in Charlie Brown shirts who look alike and wear identical fezes (a kind of hat with a tassel). Akbar and Jeff are gay, but their lives are portrayed as being little different from anyone else's since there's plenty of angst in the world to go around.

"There's a darker side of childhood that I try to make people remember. People forget how frightened kids are of adults and teenagers and big dogs and failure and other kids and all the rest, and I like to write about that."

Due to the increasing popularity of *Life In Hell*, even before it switched over to the *L.A. Weekly*, Groening was tapping other markets with it. With his then-girlfriend, Deborah (now his wife), as his business manager, she arranged to publish an oversize collection of *Life In Hell* in November 1984. The first 2,000-copy press run sold out immediately and by going back to press she was able to sell 20,000 more. They then left their respective jobs at the *Reader* (where she was in advertising) and founded the Life In Hell Co. as well as Acme Features, which syndicates *Life In Hell* and the strip of two other artists as well.

Today the company has seven employees and handles all aspects of licensing the comic strip and the characters who people it. *Life In Hell* can be found in 300 newspapers coast-to-coast. In the Eighties, a major newspaper syndicate was interested in marketing the strip for him, but said he'd have to change the name so as not to offend anyone's sensibilities. Change it to what, he wondered, "Life In Heck?"

He chose to continue marketing the strip through his own company, recognizing that a request so major would soon lead to demands that would control the writing of the strip itself. In 1986, he told *Honk* magazine, "I've been approached by daily comic syndicates off and on for the last few years. I love cartooning. I like to read good cartoons, but it's not the only thing there is in my life and I certainly can't see me sweating over a drawing board every day for the rest of my life writing something that is pasteurized enough to pass muster in the daily newspaper format."

In the years since, other collections of the strips have appeared grouped by subject into such collections as *School Is Hell*, *Childhood Is Hell*, *Work Is Hell*, *Love Is Hell* and most recently the all-encompassing *Big Book of Hell*. Readers will find them both amusing and mildly disturbing because they are so on target in their observations.

The *School Is Hell* and *Childhood Is Hell* books have a common theme of adults imposing their world view on helpless children and exercising random displays of control and power for their own sake. The reader feels once more what it was like to be in those powerless positions in childhood, and recognizes the often rampant unfairness of the situations. He also captures the political realities of the child-teacher relationship with relentless accuracy. "There's a darker side of childhood that I try to make people remember. People forget how frightened kids are of adults and teenagers and big dogs and failure and other kids and all the rest, and I like to write about that."

Groening's *Life In Hell* cartoon is somewhat of an amalgam of the single panel cartoon and the comic strip. While he does occasionally do one panel gags, more often he uses his square space to do a multi-panel strip using as many ideas in one installment as another cartoonist would use in a week of daily strips. An extreme example from the *School Is Hell* collection is the 1987 strip entitled— *Lesson 14: The 81 Types Of High School Students*, which literally has 81 panels in rows of varying numbers which, like a doctor's eye chart, get smaller as you get closer to the bottom until the panels in the last row are each smaller than your thumbnail.

The average cartoon has about 10 panels each of which suggests a different thought such as "Tips For Teens: If someone drops his or her stuff in the rush be-

"I got a number of letters from people telling me they knew exactly what God looked like," Groening told Honk magazine. "A woman named Barbara in Ohio told me she was God and that people didn't understand her because they could not understand Barbara-speak. I got letters from Hare Krishnas. I got letters from Jesus freaks who told me that I may call my strip Life In Hell but, 'you're going to Hell, dude.' So those go into a special file in case I ever show up headless in a canal nearby."

tween classes, be sure to stomp on it. An entire year's work can be trampled, ripped and destroyed in a matter of seconds if everyone cooperates." In another cartoon, entitled *Lesson 8: Trouble: Getting In And Weaseling Your Way Out Of*, one of the multiple gags in the strip is, "Very Advanced Trouble. Dropping a bag of ball bearings on the floor. Laughing at everything the teacher says. Putting snails in the teacher's briefcase. Throwing maple-syrup balloons."

Groening's cartoons are equal justice explorations of the perils of life, showing the horrors students inflict on teachers as well as the offensive positions teachers usually occupy. In *Lesson 12: High School—the 2nd Deepest Pit In Hell*, one of the gags says: "Warning! Do not talk to teachers in the same tone of voice they use talking to you. You will be suspended for insolence." In *Lesson 15: How To Get By When Yer Smarter Than Yer Teachers*, one of the warnings is, "Never Corner A Teacher. Although generally docile, teachers have been known to attack savagely when backed up against a wall. Remember teachers hate saying: 'I don't know.' And they cannot ever, ever say: 'I'm sorry.' "

To give you an idea of the variety and complexity of the several gags Groening will expend in a single cartoon, this same cartoon also includes, "Hate School??? Console yourself with this thought. At least you get to graduate and scram. Your teachers never graduate. They're stuck here," as well as the disturbing observation, "No Matter How Bad It Gets, Don't Kill Yourself!!!! They will make jokes about you. Death lasts even longer than grade school and high school put together. There is no TV in Heaven (There is TV in Hell, however.)"

When Matt Groening found the diary he kept in 1965 when in the fifth grade, he used it in several installments of *Life In Hell*, changing only the names of the other people mentioned. As a fifth grader, he had a straightforward observation of reality very much like his later writing in the strip, though not tinged with the more complicated cynicism of his adulthood.

For example, several diary entries would be used in one cartoon and one of those entries reads, "April 22, 1965. People got in trouble 26 times today. Spike N. was whispering in the library so Mr. Shute made him write a 1000-word essay. After school I went to David Weinman's birthday party. We went to the circus. It was really cool. The tiger peed on the ball and the trainer put his hand on it. I couldn't believe it."

On a more personal level: "April 23, 1965. Mr. Shute taped my mouth shut all afternoon because he saw me whispering to Freckles Jackson. Every one laughed when he put the tape on. I guess that is why he did it, to make me feel stupid."

Matt kept getting into trouble with Mr. Shute. One of the best entries recalling the indignities he endured reads, "April 30, 1965. Mr. Shute got so mad today he threw some chalk at Spike. Spike ducked. I got in trouble so during recess I had to stand in the corner under the shed. I didn't have anything to do so I taught myself to blow spit bubbles off the end of my tongue."

While these and other *Life In Hell* installments dealing with school were running in the *L.A. Weekly* in the mid-Eighties, not all readers appreciated them. Some thought they were too cute, preferring Groening's more trenchant humor as he applied it to his observations about modern times. What these critics failed to appreciate was the fact that what Groening was describing about grade school, high school, etc., was by no means ancient history. The strangeness he was relating in those cartoons concerned things someone somewhere was experiencing even as we were reading about them. Some things don't change very much, or at all.

Life In Hell remains a huge canvas on which to draw his ideas, and Groening is just happy that he's allowed to ex-

CONCLUSION

MY 5th GRADE DIARY

PART EIGHT
BY MATT GROENING

May 20, 1965
Today at school oh shoot I can't write with this dumb pencil.
May 21, 1965
Shoot, I see the spelling isn't so good in this journal. You may not believe this but I am a great speller. Its just that when I'm tired I don't spell good. Crust, I got in trouble today for groaning. Mr. Shute got mad so I get kicked out of the room. Isn't that dumb?!?? Oh, well. Sorry for me. Until I write again I remain.
Matt Groening

May 24, 1965
I decided I'll never be prez of the U.S. so I think I'll stop now.
June 10, 1965
I think I'll start again. Lotsa cool jazz has happened since May 24, but I can't remember all of them. Mr. Shute sure is a bunch of swear words. A couple of days ago he gave me a 1000 word essay on the History of Football. For no reason. Other essays were Life cycle of the whale, Animal life on the Sahara

desert, witchcraft, The Fuedal Castle, life of Beethoven, diamond mining. You turn it in and he rips it up. Isn't that crusty? Yesterday these guys came over to our school from another to celebrate that they got out of school for the summer. They had these BB guns and they were shooting guys. Melvin and Fartface got hit. Then Mr. Love called the fuzz and they came and hauled em off to Junior Disneyland Hotel. If ya don't know what that means think of J.D.H. Today was the last day of school.

It was the coolest deal ya ever seed. After school me and Spike were really heaving all these water balloons all over. Then these guys came along and heaved about 10 at us. Also I told ya about the party for Shute. The girls didn't have enough money to buy him a radio so they got him sum pencils. Mr. Shute wouldn't let Spike have any refreshments but he had em anyway.
P.S. Looking back at the whole school year I have but one thing to say-- I HATE MR. SHUTE!
P.S. again. I AM FREE!!!!!

plore them his way without interference. "Taboos have loosened up. Thirty years ago you couldn't do strips on death, snakes or body odor."

In the collection *Childhood Is Hell*, the world outside the classroom is tackled with equally ascerbic fervor. In a 1988 installment, one of the dozen gags in that particular strip (called *Your Pal The TV Set*) reads: "Why Is TV So Cool? It allows several people who hate each other's guts to sit peacefully together in the same room for years on end without murdering each other." I guess this is what Donald Wildman and his cronies mean when they talk about wanting television which preserves family values.

On the same childhood theme, he did a strip called *What Does God Look Like?* and asked his friends what they thought God looked like when they were kids. The ideas ranged from God looking like someone's grandfather to another thinking he looked like Santa Claus. Matt himself thought that perhaps God looked like the flaming head from *The Wizard of Oz*.

"I got a number of letters from people telling me they knew exactly what God looked like," Groening told *Honk* magazine. "A woman named Barbara in Ohio told me *she* was God and that people didn't understand her because they could not understand Barbara-speak. I got letters from Hare Krishnas, I got letters from Jesus freaks who told me that I may call my strip *Life In Hell* but, 'you're going to Hell, dude.' So those go into a special file in case I ever show up headless in a canal nearby."

In 1986 Groening created the characters which eventually would bring him more recognition in two years than *Life In Hell* brought him in 10. *The Simpsons* (named after his father and sisters, with Bart being an anagram for brat) were created in Groening's highly recognizable style and animated in two minute shorts which ran on Fox Television's *The Tracy Ullman Show* beginning on the third episode in April, 1987.

Looking at these early versions of the characters, consistency is not a hallmark. The look of the characters occasionally changes, including having Bart rendered as an older teenager in some. They were popular within the confines of *The Tracy Ullman Show* so Fox decided to transfer them to their own half-hour series. Some believed they wouldn't translate well to the longer format, but when the series premiered in 1990, it became the proverbial overnight success and soon *everyone* was talking about *The Simpsons*.

Anyone familiar with *Life In Hell* could see Groening's writing style and sensibilities all through the show and its characters. Under the production guidance of James L. Brooks, the level of writing on the series has remained remarkably high, and executive producer Sam Simon also contributes creatively to the shaping of the series and the approach taken to the characters. Secondary characters in the series were created by two of the animation directors, David Silverman and Wesley Archer.

A jazz saxophonist, Bleeding Gums Murphy, who has appeared in at least two episodes, was created by Simon. Groening still oversees production of key aspects of the series and Simpsons merchandise has literally flooded the market. Says Groening, "I don't own *The Simpsons*, but I do get to steer the all-terrain vehicle."

Although referred to as the epitome of a dysfunctional American family, this seems to be what many people like about them. Unlike most other sitcom families, the trials and tribulations of these rather ugly, animated characters strike a far more realistic pose than families on television normally convey in sitcoms. While TV is overrun with smart-mouthed kids, not unlike Bart Simpson, those around Bart seldom laugh at his antics. They often respond with threats, intimidation and even outright attempts at violence, just like real people would when confronted with such a little hellion.

Reaction to the series was so overwhelming in early 1990 that, in a move virtually unprecedented for Fox, they called a halt to allowing interviews about the series for fear that it would become over-exposed in the press. It was cover featured on a variety of magazines, including *Newsweek* (April 23, 1990), *Entertainment Weekly* (May 18, 1990) and *The Los Angeles Times Magazine* (April 29, 1990) as well as in most major and minor newspapers around the country.

The show itself has lampooned its own success. On the 1990 Thanksgiving episode Bart complains that none of his favorite new cartoon characters are featured in the Macy's Thanksgiving Day parade on TV. Homer remarks, "If you start building a balloon for every flash-in-the pan cartoon character, you turn the parade into a farce!" Just then a Bart Simpson balloon floats across the screen for a split second just as a real Bart Simpson balloon did that day in New York City.

The show itself has lampooned its own success. On the 1990 Thanksgiving episode Bart complains that none of his favorite new cartoon characters are featured in the Macy's Thanksgiving Day parade on TV. Homer remarks, "If you start building a balloon for every flash-in-the pan cartoon character, you turn the parade into a farce!" Just then a Bart Simpson balloon floats across the screen for a split second just as a real Bart Simpson balloon did that day in New York City.

Groening's writing style infuses the show, particular in some of the dialogue. Anyone familiar with *Life In Hell* would not be at all surprised with lines of dialogue such as the one Homer Simpson spoke in the episode in which he took a sassy foreign exchange student into his home. When Lisa gets into an argument with the boy, Homer admonishes her with, "Now, now, Lisa, you're right. Democracy is wonderful, but maybe our little guest has a point here when he says that the machinery of capitalism is greased with the blood of the workers." While it sounds like a very unlikely thing for the dim-witted Homer to say, we accept it because he's been shown to have a horrible job working for a sleazy boss in a nuclear power plant.

Rather than being a typical sitcom whose plots are just skeletons upon which to hang jokes, *The Simpsons* goes beyond that. It often explores the characters with something sitcoms long since seem to have abandoned: subtlety. The thankful absence of an annoying laughtrack enables the audience to decide whether something is funny or not, just as we do when we go to a theater.

Clearly, not everyone appreciates *The Simpsons*, and just as some are put off by *Life In Hell*, others are upset by *The Simpsons* for very different reasons as revealed just recently in the Sunday news magazine *USA Weekend*. They invited readers to tell how their family was like *The Simpsons*. Along with a lot of amusing replies, it prompted some sour grapes as well, including the following.

"As a teacher of elementary school-aged children, I am deeply concerned and offended at your 'Real-Life Simpsons' contest. Children today need positive role models and heroes." Robyn Wisdom, Bishop, Calif.

and. . .

"Asking families to compete to be like a dysfunctional cartoon family is a gross disservice to the American home. In this time of drug use, teen pregnancy, lowered educational achievement and broken homes, we should be encouraging love, caring and educational growth. No, my family is not like The Simpsons, thank God. I hope The Cosby Show runs this social blight off the television." Sydney Fulbright, Fort Smith, Ark.

Other people have found completely different things to complain about. A representative of the nuclear power industry criticized the portrayal of Homer Simpson as a bumbling nuclear plant worker who acts oblivious to safety precautions. The producers of *The Simpsons* have promised that in the future they'll needle the nuclear power industry more responsibly. This will include Homer saying grace before a meal by stating, "Thank you for nuclear power, which has yet to cause a single fatality, at least in this country."

Homer also will prevent a nuclear meltdown at the plant when he wakes up during the crisis, by chance pushes just the right button to avert disaster and thereafter feels guilty about being a hero. On the other hand, the producers have promised not to do any more episodes about mutant, three-eyed fish, as though a cartoon sitcom is supposed to be a cold reflection of reality. That anyone would take anything in *The Simpsons* that seriously shows a misplaced perception of what is and isn't important.

Matt Groening has found that even among those who should be his critics, there are fans. When the cartoonist was recognized while walking past a Los Angeles movie theater where a group of Christians were picketing the film *Jesus of Montreal*, some of the children who'd been brought along to swell the ranks of the protestors ran up to Groening, demanding his autograph. "They wanted me to autograph the T-shirts they were wearing, as long as I didn't write any of the bad words Bart sometimes says."

Groening's approach to comedy in general, and not just *The Simpsons* in particular, can perhaps be exemplified in a comment he made regarding one of his installments of *Life In Hell*, the strip he still draws each week in spite of his daily workload with *The Simpsons*.

"One week I put in a line about Akbar and Jeff being brothers or lovers or possibly both; and sometime later I came up with a strip in which the revelation that indeed they most likely were gay was part of the punchline. It turns out it was a real good decision; I got lots of people real excited about it and it perturbed a number of other people, which makes me happy. If I can make somebody laugh and really annoy the hell out of someone else, I think I've done my job."

LIFE IN HELL

© 1987 BY MATT GROENING

SCHOOL IS HELL

THE LINGERING EFFECTS OF HAVING ONE'S CARTOONS CONFISCATED IN THE 6th GRADE

LESSON 9: HOW TO DRIVE A DESERVING TEACHER CRAZY

3 ANNOYING WAYS TO ASK TO GO TO THE LAVATORY

- MAY I GO TO THE LABORATORY?
- MAY I GO TO THE LABRADOR?
- MAY I GO SEE THE LAVA FLOW?

BELA LUGOSI ACCENT

DON'T ALL TEACHERS DESERVE TO BE DRIVEN CRAZY?

STRANGELY, THE ANSWER IS NO. WE MUST REMEMBER THAT TEACHERS USED TO BE SMALL AND SPEEDY, JUST LIKE US. BUT THEN THEY GREW UP, GOT SOPHISTICATED, AND WENT SENILE.

IF THEY ARE NICE AND FUNNY AND TEACH US A THING OR TWO, THEN WE SHOULD TAKE PITY ON THE POOR UNDERPAID DRUDGES AND GIVE 'EM A BREAK. UNLESS WE'RE IN A RAMBUNCTIOUS MOOD.

HOW TO TELL IF A TEACHER DESERVES TO BE DRIVEN CRAZY
A CHECKLIST

- ☐ CALLS ON YOU WHEN YOU ARE SCRUNCHED DOWN IN YOUR SEAT TRYING TO LOOK AS INCONSPICUOUS AS POSSIBLE.
- ☐ LOCKS THE CLASSROOM DOOR WHEN THE BELL RINGS AND WON'T OPEN UP NO MATTER HOW HARD YOU KICK
- ☐ NEVER SMILES
- ☐ SMILES TOO MUCH
- ☐ PUNISHES YOU UNFAIRLY
- ☐ PUNISHES YOU FAIRLY

MAKING A CRAZY TEACHER CRAZIER—THE CYCLE

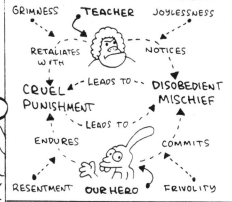

GRIMNESS · · · TEACHER · · · JOYLESSNESS

RETALIATES WITH · · · NOTICES

CRUEL PUNISHMENT - -LEADS TO- - DISOBEDIENT MISCHIEF

- -LEADS TO-

ENDURES · · · COMMITS

RESENTMENT · OUR HERO · FRIVOLITY

SMALL WAYS TO DRIVE A DESERVING TEACHER CRAZY

- PRETEND YOU AREN'T LISTENING.
- ASK DISTRACTING QUESTIONS.
- SAY: "COULD YOU REPEAT THAT?"
- ACT STUPID.

MEDIUM-SIZED WAYS TO DRIVE A DESERVING TEACHER CRAZY

- HIDE ALL THE BLACKBOARD ERASERS.
- MAKE LITTLE MEOWING NOISES WITHOUT MOVING YOUR LIPS.
- ACT SMART.

BIG WAYS TO DRIVE A DESERVING TEACHER CRAZY

- SQUIRT WATER ON THE TEACHER'S CHAIR WHEN SHE ISN'T LOOKING.
- SMUGGLE AS MANY DOGS AS YOU CAN INTO THE CLASSROOM.
- SAY THINGS THAT MAKE THE CLASS LAUGH BUT WHICH THE TEACHER DOESN'T GET.

IF YOU GET KICKED OUT OF CLASS, YOU CAN STILL DRIVE A DESERVING TEACHER CRAZY

1. GATHER YOUR STUFF AS SLOWLY AS POSSIBLE.
2. WALK SOLEMNLY TOWARD THE DOOR. AT THE LAST MOMENT, TWIRL.
3. SLAM THE DOOR AND MAKE GOOFY FACES IN THE LITTLE WINDOW. THEN RUN.
4. WAIT 20 YEARS, THEN DRAW A BOOK OF SNOTTY CARTOONS ABOUT SCHOOL.

DOOP DE DOO

MOTHER GOOSE AND GRIMM

Mike Peters has been a popular political cartoonist for more than 20 years, but six years ago he chose to expand his horizons and created the daily comic strip Mother Goose & Grimm. While usually about a dog, it sometimes strays into totally unrelated territories of humor and fantasy.

By James Van Hise

"**I**'ve been drawing all my life," Mike Peters said from his home in Florida. "I started when I was a little kid. I was one of those class clowns and also a terrible student. Plus I had a real bad stutter so I had a hard time communicating with people, and especially meeting girls. So I would draw in order to communicate, in a sense. I started drawing when I was 5 or 6 years old." By the time he was 13, he was taking his portfolio of cartoons around to businesses looking for work as a cartoonist. That's enthusiasm.

"I loved to draw. I loved the process and I loved the idea," Peters continued. "I started doing a bunch of cartoons for my grade school, and then in high school, too. Then I started going around to local newspapers and magazines. We had a couple of teen magazines in my area. One was *Prom* magazine. I took my cartoons in there and a couple of them were printed. I took a bunch of my cartoons into one newspaper, the *Webster Kirkwood Advertiser*, when I was about 15 and they started using them on a regular basis, once a week." These were editorial cartoons about Webster Groves, Mo., right outside St. Louis, where Mike Peters grew up.

"I was ecstatic when they printed my first cartoon," Peters recalled. "So I'd been doing that all through high school and college. I did regular cartoons for a Catholic newspaper called the *St. Loluis Review*. One summer I did a batch of cartoons and took them around to local radio stations." These cartoons showed the dog, Tony, that Mike had as a youth. "It was a cocker spaniel and I drew it very Disneyesque, with cute little eyes, and it was lying around a radio." Two or three of these were published by the radio station in advertisements in the *Post-Dispatch*.

"I'd gone to college at Washington University in St. Louis to go through art school, and by the time I was a junior I had a huge portfolio of published cartoons. And these weren't just published in the school newspaper," Peters explained, "but in five or six other publications on a regular basis."

When Mike was a child, he loved the comics page in the newspaper and prided himself on knowing the name of every cartoonist on the comic page. He read both *Pogo* and Peanuts back in the Fifties when they began.

"I knew I wanted to be a cartoonist then, but I didn't know what kind," Peters said. "I started out thinking I was going to be an animator. I love animation. I grew up watching Warner Brothers cartoons in the theatres, even before they hit television. And when Disneyland became popular on TV I was always watching that. Then I thought about doing comic strips, but I didn't know any comic strip cartoonists and I didn't think I had that ability."

When Mike was growing up, his mother had a TV show in St. Louis called *The Charlotte Peters Show* from 1948 to about 1968. Mike drew cartoons for her program. He sometimes would do illustrattions for something she was reading or songs she would sing. Mike even appeared on the show occasionally doing things, but he never drew on the air. He said his wife saw him for the first time when he was 10 and appeared on the show.

"My mom was a real interesting lady and she's who I kind of took Mother Goose from. She worked for the NBC affiliate, owned by Pulitzer, and in '58 Bill Mauldin came to take over for P.R. Fitzpatrick, editorial cartoonist for the *Post-Dispatch*. Bill Mauldin had gotten his name for doing Willy and Joe in World War II, but then when the war was over in '45, he tried to keep it going but people didn't want to be reminded of the war and his syndication fell way off."

Mauldin's first attempts at editorial cartooning didn't pan out but he made a comeback eight years later when Fitzpatrick retired and Mauldin won a Pulitzer Prize the following year. "I had seen his cartoons," Peters said, "and when he won the Pulitzer, people wrote a lot of stories about him and I knew that this is what I wanted to be when I grew up."

One day Mike's mother took him down to meet Mauldin. "And for the next two years, until he left for Chicago, I'd go in to see him every two or three months, and he'd let me sit there and watch him draw. I was very influenced by him."

When Mike Peters got out of college he began looking for jobs as a cartoonist. He was close to landing one at the St. Louis *Post-Dispatch,* but that didn't work out. "That was a big turning point in my life because if I had gotten the job there I probably would have stayed in St. Louis for the rest of my life.

"I had decided that I wanted to be an editorial cartoonist," Peters said. "I saw that as a means for me to really educate myself about the world. That was an education that I felt that I had not taken advantage of when I was in school because I was such a terrible student. So I got on a train and went to Chicago and they had about six newspapers up there at the time. I tried all those papers and they were very nice. The one that had an art staff that I felt I was in sync with was the *Chicago Daily News*. They seemed to be impressed by my portfolio, but they weren't hiring at the time."

Peters was in the building, standing at the elevator, preparing to leave, when he looked over and saw the office of Bill Mauldin. Mike had seen him there once or twice before, but had never asked him for a favor before, and in fact had never even shown Mauldin his cartoon work.

"All those years that I'd known him I'd been afraid to show him my cartoons because I thought, God, if he doesn't like them I'm going to be so crushed that I'd probably go into another profession." But Mike had graduated from college and he really wanted to find work as a cartoonist. He told Mauldin that the art staff on the *Chicago Daily News* liked Mike's work but that they didn't need anyone at the time. "Bill called up the editor and said, 'I'm sending a kid down, I want you to take a look at him.' I went down and met the editor, Mr. Fanning, showed him my cartoons and he hired me."

Two and a half years later, after Peters had been drafted, been in the Army for a year and then returned to the newspaper, Bill Mauldin walked in one day and said, "I was talking to an editor in Dayton, Ohio and he wants to see your stuff." Mike Peters was hired as an editorial cartoonist and maintains that job to this day, even though the cartoonist and his family relocated to Florida a few years ago.

Not many editorial cartoonists also draw comic strips. Mike Peters is one and Jeff MacNelly (*Shoe*) is another. For some reason, the two branches of cartooning tend not to cross over very often. But on two occasions in the past 20 years, the Pulitzer Prize for political cartoon commentary went to comic strips, and both times most of the editorial cartoonists reacted quite negatively, a view not shared by Mike Peters.

"I thought it was hysterical the reaction that editorial cartoonists had when *Doonesbury* won and later when *Bloom County* won. These strips, and I think *Doonesbury* more than *Bloom County*, are very political. I think *Bloom County* was very much social commentary, and the Pulitzer Prize is for commentary. So I thought it was a riot.

"When *Doonesbury* won, the Editorial Cartoonists Association was run by what I thought was a bunch of old (fogeys)," Peters continued. "And when they said that they're upset about *Doonesbury*, I just thought, well... these are guys who are locked into a certain system and so they could not deal with the fact that good commentary was being done by someone who was being printed on the comics page. But then when *Bloom County* won, about a decade later, the Editorial Cartoonists Association was being run by young guys. And these weren't old (guys); these were guys that are younger than I am! But it got the

> "All those years that I'd known him I'd been afraid to show him my cartoons because I thought, God, if he doesn't like them I'm going to be so crushed that I'd probably go into another profession."

same reaction, and that's when I thought... these are just guys who cannot take the fact that their little kingdom is being superceded by guys on the comic page.

For sure, *Doonesbury* and *Bloom County* deserved that award because they were doing good commentary. And there are so many other guys who have done great commentary who have not been given that award. This does not take anything away from *Doonesbury* or *Bloom County*, but just because they're in another area, and they're not necessarily Editorial Cartoonists with a capital 'E,' people want to overlook them. David Levine did some fabulous work in the Sixties, and was completely overlooked. Jules Feiffer has been doing political and social commentary in his comic strip 'Feiffer' for decades, and he was only just acknowledged five or six years ago."

WE WARNED HIM NOT TO CROSS THE PICKET LINE...

It was 14 years after he began drawing political cartoons as a living for the *Dayton Daily News* that Peters decided he wanted to do something else as well.

"The reason why I started doing the strip was that I needed to have a certain amount of pressure put on myself because I had done the same job for the same company for a long time. I had turned down a bunch of newspapers who offered to have me move and work for them because I was raising kids and I liked the lifestyle in Dayton. We had all of our friends in Dayton. I was going to a great church in Dayton. But most important, I loved the people at the Cox newspapers. They always treated me wonderfully. Cox newspapers are a very special group," Peters stressed.

"They are a family-oriented company and they're just very decent with you, and I found that that is a rare commodity in lots of businesses. So whenever the opportunities would come up, I'd just say no. I wouldn't even take the time to go to the places and hear what they had to say. But the problem with that is that editorial cartoonists don't grow up to be editors, they grow up to be old editorial cartoonists. So what happens is when you do the same job for 14 or 15 years and everybody is loving it and you're working for a wonderful company, I didn't have any pressure. I just did not have the pressure that you need to have when you do a job like this.

"I cannot think of one editorial cartoonist who has been with one newspaper for his whole career. While there may be one, what most editorial cartoonists do is work at one paper for five or 10 years and then they move to another newspaper. I think they make that move less for money and more to put pressure on themselves. You've got a new boss. You've got someone who has gone out of their way to get you and bring you into this town for you to fulfill a function as a hired gun or whatever they hire editorial cartoonists for. Then you have that pressure of, 'Oh, I hope I do them a good job! I'm gonna' show them that they made the right choice!' That's pressure."

Mike Peters didn't want to leave the *Dayton Daily News*. He'd made the decision to remain with the paper but felt he needed to put new creative pressure on himself.

"I had been showing my editorial cartoons on the *Today Show* for three or four years, and what that was doing was getting me a lot of speaking engagements at colleges and the like. While I made some extra money that way, I hated traveling. So I decided that if I'm going to stick with the *Daily News*, and I don't want to travel, but I need to put pressure on myself, the perfect way is by trying to start a comic strip. And so once I decided I wanted to do that, I immediately knew that I wanted to use this dog that I had drawn for many years because I've always related myself to dogs.

"Dogs are inherently funny to me even though there are *12 billion dogs* in comic strips. I did not set out saying, 'Hmm, there's not a pirate strip, so I'll do a pirate strip.' They always say that what you should do is find that void and then fill it with something. But that didn't interest me. If I was going to do a strip, I was going to do a strip about something that I'm interested in or something that I feel something about.

"I love dogs," Peters added. "I think they're just basically funny. I love them because I relate to them. They never think about what they look like. They just let it hang out. They lick themselves at the wrong time and at terrible spots, like in front of crowds. They can't hold their emotions. If they're hungry they will break into a trash can and start eating. If they're happy, you can tell it because they're wagging their tail hysterically and they can't stop themselves from wagging.

"I have Grimm trying to do that all the time: *'God, I hate being so obvious, so predictable!'* And that's me! If someone is talking and I get an idea I go, 'Wait! Let me just tell you my idea!' I have all these terrible flaws and I think the reason I love dogs is that it's the same type of things that dogs do.

"So I knew I wanted to do a strip about a dog," Peters continued, "but I didn't want it to be a dog strip, although as it's turned into a dog strip. But my biggest fear was, Oh, God, I don't want to be doing a 'Fred Basset.' Lots of dog collar jokes and stuff like that. So I had this dog but I didn't know what I wanted to do."

What Mike Peters did then was take all of his own favorites of the editorial cartoons he'd drawn and spread about 50 of them out on the floor in order to try to perceive from his own work what he liked doing best.

"I found that what I liked doing was animals and fantasy. I had a lot of analogies to Dis-

"The reason why I started doing the strip was that I needed to have a certain amount of pressure put on myself because I had done the same job for the same company for a long time. "

ney characters and such," Peters stated. "I don't do that much any more in my editorial cartoons, but at the time I would often have Snow White doing something about the federal budget or some such. Cartoons that are just cute as hell! They make me sick now, but at the time I thought they were just adorable. And so I decided that since I like animals and I like fantasy, I'll put the dog in that kind of environment."

The first thing he tried was to put the dog with Robinson Crusoe.

"Here's a fantasy-kind of character; a literary character and it's fun having the combination of the old grinchy man and this dog. I did that for a couple of weeks until I realized I was just doing coconut jokes and so I hated that. Now this isn't a fantasy idea, but I put the dog on the street with a bag lady and I liked that for a couple of weeks. The bag lady was kind of gruff, just like the old man was and the dog is kind of gruff. It's like a bull terrier, and so they don't compliment each other. So I

"I was greatly influenced by The Far Side," Peters admitted. "Gary Larson was tapping something brand new in the way he was putting characters together."

tried a whole bunch of different things and nothing was working, and then I looked in a Mother Goose book to try to find different nursery rhymes to think about and all of a sudden I realized, Mother Goose! Here's this little lady that could be sweet and yet have a dark side to her, much like my mom. I drew Mother Goose much like I did the bag lady, and then I put the two together and it seemed to work. But most important to me, the thing I enjoyed was that if I do this, I don't have to do just a dog strip. And if I call it *Mother Goose & Grimm* (from the Brothers Grimm), then I can do anything I want to do.

"I was greatly influenced by *The Far Side*," Peters admitted. "Gary Larson was tapping something brand new in the way he was putting characters together. So then I started really doing two different kinds of strips. One with absolutely generic ideas that I thought were just fun; things that made me laugh. And then strips of the dog and Mother Goose, and I did them equally for about two years. All the dog strips were either single panel or four panel gags that were single gags to themselves, and I was having a wonderful time and it was fun, but I wasn't learning very much.

It's the same kind of pattern as editorial cartoons because it's a single panel, totally remote from any other panel that you do. It tells a simple story one way or the other, and it was about two years into it that I started really to tap myself, and going through my experiences and my fears and my joys and started putting them down in the strip. First I decided that I wanted the dog to date, and once I did that, the strip started taking on a totally different kind of character and something that I've been doing now for the last three or four years, and I love it! I'm having a ball because I'm in a brand new playing field. I've never done this before. And it is really a stitch. I'm really having a good time.

"I love when I put the dog into a series where he gets himself stuck in some kind of situation," Peters explained. "And that emotion that I get from this situation is just pure me! It's like a little novel that I write that goes for two, three or four weeks. But that little novel is tapping something in me that I've never tapped before. Editorial cartoons are third person. Single panel gags are mostly third person. But when you put a character into a series and you have him or her deal with some sort of relationship, or deal with some sort of fear, such as school or dating. That's tapping something inside you, and that's what I love. That's why I love doing the comic strip."

While Mike Peters draws political cartoons five days a week for the *Dayton Daily News*, his work in *Mother Goose & Grimm* is completely different, but he explained that he doesn't consciously avoid doing political gags in the comic strip. "I just don't think it's appropriate for the dog. But I think that if I were not doing my editorial cartoons, I think that the comic strip would probably be very political. But because I have my outlet on that, then I don't feel the need to be doing politics, mainly because I'm having too much fun doing what I'm doing right now."

"Let's say that if I ever got bored doing this, and I can see looking back over my career that when I get bored, that's when I change. Or to put it another way, when I find something that excites me, I go in that direction. But I'm having so much fun tapping these things in me that I've never tapped before, that I have no need of having Grimm be political."

On the other hand, Peters revealed that he just happened to be working on a story line for the comic strip which would have some mild political overtones while still keeping within the recognizable parameters of *Mother Goose & Grimm*.

"I'm starting a story in the strip right now where he's going to be in kind of a political situation. Mother Goose is going to take him on a trip and he's going to escape from her and be running around Washington and he's going to meet a little spaniel and fall in love with her, and it'll turn out to be Millie, the White House dog. I see

MOTHER GOOSE & GRIMM By Mike Peters

LET'S SEE....HE MUST'VE BEEN TEN, ELEVEN, TWELVE YEARS OLD....

in my mind that he's going to be chased around the White House by the Secret Service and it's going to be fun.

"That could be a political cartoon, and yet I don't have any desire to have it be a political thing. I see it as a funny situation because of Mrs. Bush's book, which I've read and it kind of made me gag but I'd like to try to use some of the stuff from there inside the comic strip."

Among the modern humor strips on the newspaper comics page, Peters mentions a number as being among his personal favorites.

"Gary Larson's *The Far Side* is great. *Bloom County* is wonderful and I'm sure he's going to be coming back with it. I love *Calvin & Hobbes*, and *Shoe*. Those are usually the first things that I read. There are other strips that I get to, but those are the ones that excite me when I read them."

Regarding the different trends in humor which have been explored on the comics page, Peters observed, "During the time of Vietnam is when *Doonesbury* came around. That's when he became accepted and widely syndicated. But what I feel is that probably the thing that has influenced most of the comic pages in newspapers is *Saturday Night Live*. SNL brought a certain dark humor into the mainstream, and that dark humor has overlapped into *Far Side* and *Bloom County* and *Doonesbury* and that made it accepted by that group who traditionally, when they read the comic pages, thought it was going to be mainly white bread stuff. The kind of stuff you might see in the *Saturday Evening Post* or the humor section in *Reader's Digest*. But *Saturday Night Live* made it acceptable to do slam cartoons. Humor with an edge. And that's made it very exciting for me.

"I can see just in the fairly brief career of the *Mother Goose & Grimm* strip, when I was just starting out, I got just terrible letters about things that I was doing that I thought were basically funny. What people are bothered by is never what you hope they're going to be bothered by. In my editorial cartooning career, you always hope that they're going to be upset about the the issue rather than the way you portray it. And what they're upset about is something like, 'You should never draw a cat like that!' And you go, oh, God, what's wrong with these people!

"I didn't think that I was going to get bad letters when I drew the comic strip because they're fairly innocent. Comic strips are only to make you laugh and not really to make you angry. But without a doubt, the comic strips that really make me laugh, I'll get three or four bad letters on. For instance, I did a Sunday strip a few months ago and I just loved it. It was making a social statement, but the letters I got were taking the strip exactly opposite.

"I had Mother Goose asking the dog to help her with the dishes, and he says, *'Hey, I'm a guy! Guys don't dry dishes, and guys don't make beds and guys don't sweep up. In fact guys aren't supposed to do anything that girls do!'* And she says, *'Oh, yeah? Then why do guys have nipples?'* And Grimm just stood there and in the last panel he still hadn't moved and it's nighttime and the moon is up. It's a wonderful cartoon! But I got three letters saying, 'How could you say that guys don't do these things! There's been the whole Feminist movement and yet the cartoon said... ' Of course guys are supposed to be doing these things!

"The thing that started me having Grimm be the main character was that I wanted him to be a real dog," Peters stressed. "Something that chased cars and had fleas and ate out of trash cans and drank out of toilets! That's part and parcel of a dog. But for three or four years in the comic strip, every time I had the dog drink out of a toilet I'd lose cities! Whole cities! Every time I'd have the dog drinking out of the toilet I'd lose Pittsburg or Muncie. These editors say, 'We can't have dogs drinking out of toilets.'

"If they go to my cartoon and read it and then they go to something else without a chuckle or hitting the guy next to him and pointing to it or something like that, then that's an absolute failure, and I'll be depressed for a couple of hours afterwards. It used to depress me for a whole day. What's wrong with me! But it's that physical reaction that I'm looking for."

"I recently did a week and a half of the dog trying not to drink out of a toilet and I didn't get one bad letter on it! I only got good letters. So I think I've finally desensitized the readers about that. But it's just so funny how upset they get about the cartoons that I physically laugh at."

Peters explained that he tries to use himself as the gauge for his cartoons as to whether they succeed, and he wants to make the cartoon more than just a passive amusement. "Did I make myself laugh when I thought of that idea? In my editorial cartoons I try to either get irony, anger or laughter, but I try to make it so that I can physically get somebody to go *whoaaa!* or *Ha!* or *You can't say that!* or something! Ninety-nine percent of the stuff we see in the newspaper, whether on the comics page or the editorial page, you will look at the cartoon, read it, understand it and then go to something else. When someone does that to my cartoon, just look at it, understand it and go somewhere else, it's a failure."

When he has the opportunity, Peters likes to observe people reading the newspaper to see whether they have a reaction to his cartoons. "It's not that I go around the cities and sit there watching people read my cartoons, but I'll know when someone's reading a newspaper and they'll get to the comic page and I'll think *I'm in there.*

"If they go to my cartoon and read it and then they go to something else without a chuckle or hitting the guy next to him and pointing to it or something like that, then that's an absolute failure, and I'll be depressed for a couple of hours afterwards. It used to depress me for a whole day. *What's wrong with me!* But it's that physical reaction that I'm looking for."

Special thanks to the Tribune Media Services for arranging this interview with Mike Peters.

MOTHER GOOSE

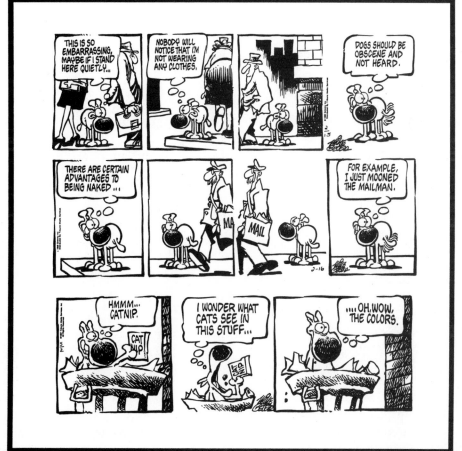

105

Comic strips about kids have been a mainstay for many years, but not until the Seventies did one come along which dealt honestly with a kid's life as seen from a kid's viewpoint. Its influence on strips which followed is quite apparent.

All visuals this chapter © 1991 by Gahan Wilson.

by James Van Hise

One of the reasons that *Calvin and Hobbes* has become so popular is that it successfully captures the way a child thinks about the world around him. Dwarfed by the world's rules and responsibilities, Calvin strikes back by exaggerating elements of it in order to deal with reality as he perceives it on his own terms. In a very different way, Matt Groening's *Life In Hell* portrays his characters grappling with reality, albeit it without the shield of fantasy to sustain them. The children of *Life In Hell* suffer and endure, greeting each new conflict with a kind of iron resignation. They don't wonder whether it could be any worse because what they're already having to deal with is bad enough.

A comic strip which I believe was the first to deal with childhood fears with brutal honesty (of the kind done later and just as well by *Life In Hell*) is Gahan Wilson's comic strip *Nuts*. It ran in the magazine *National Lampoon* during its heyday of the Seventies, when it was considered an influential and must-read publication.

The title of the strip is an obvious takeoff on the name of Charles Schultz's strip, *Peanuts*. Interestingly, Schultz never named his own strip that. The syndicate did, and he felt at the time that it was an awful name for a comic strip because it didn't reflect what the strip was in any way. In the case of *Nuts*, the title does, I think, fit the reality portrayed in the strip because it is undoubtedly our world as many of us saw it when we were small children growing up and coming to terms with life's nasty twists and turns.

Nuts is about the daily trials and tribulations of a small boy and it's told from his point of view. It captures the sense of helpless desperation children feel when confronting the randomness of life and it portrays the child's growing awareness of his own powerlessness in a world controlled by adults. Adults aren't the enemy so much as they're among the players, the tools of fate which seem to delight in tormenting the child.

The very first strip opens with this observation: "Those of you who remember how great it was to be a little kid, gang, don't remember how it was to be a little kid...." It then goes on to portray what it was like when you were sick as a kid, and how awful it really was. Since this strip began in the early Seventies, the author was re-calling sensations and experiences from his own childhood, which even included the now forgotten concept of a doctor making a house call. The nameless child in the strip re-calls the doctor's visit in the following way.

DOCTOR: Yeah, well the kid does have something... you call Smith's drugstore, don't call any other drugstore, and buy what I tell you. Does it hurt here? (prods the child with a huge finger)

MOTHER: Is he going to die, doctor?

DOCTOR: No, I don't think so—but those are some germs he's got—need a lot of medicine from Smith's.

Since things are not only remembered as being very dramatic to a child, they seem very dramatic to a child at the time. This little boy imagines he can see the monstrous germs in his fever dream and one of them is saying, "We're going to kill you, kid!"

Wilson's strip is one of those joys in which the story and the art are of equal importance, and Wilson's art has a crude individuality which communicates an intensity through his line and a grimness of purpose few others have ever come close to. I can only compare it with the work of Charles Addams and Edward Gorey.

Wilson could also recall the joys as well as the terrors of childhood, such as what visiting grandparents was like. In one such strip he begins: "Remember how different really old people were from people only as old as your parents? And how it seemed to be easier for them to talk to kids, and you to them?"

Even comic books got a sidebar on Wilson's memory lane.

"Remember how terrific the comic books were? All the swell, exciting stuff that was in them? And wondering why it was only kids seemed to realize they were great?"

(The kid and his friend are standing in a small store reading through the latest comic books.)

THE KID: Boy—this Captain Power is really great, isn't he? And that rocket of his is something!

THE KID'S FRIEND: He's plenty good, but I like Doctor Science and his lab and all!

THE KID: Gee, here he's on Mars and caught by the walking mushrooms!

MR. SCHULTZ: Are you kids going to buy one of those?

THE KID'S FRIEND: Yeah, but look here where Doctor Science has accidentally got shrunk and the evil professor's got him in a bottle!

MR. SCHULTZ: This is a business, not a library!

THE KID: Here you are Mr. Schultz.

THE KID'S FRIEND: Here you are Mr. Schultz.

MR. SCHULTZ: High time.

THE KID'S FRIEND: It's funny how Mr. Schultz is such a grumpy person. You'd think he'd be happy with all those great books around.

THE KID: Maybe he doesn't really appreciate them.

As idyllic as this is, much of *Nuts* deals with the more frightening aspects of growing up that the other kids strips up to this time studiously avoided. For instance, there's the strip which begins: "Remember the first time you saw a grown-up really being sick? I mean really, really sick? And how scary it was because now you knew that nothing was invulnerable?"

It shows the kid visiting his Uncle Jack in the hospital. While his uncle looks okay at first, when he starts coughing he can't stop and the coughs get worse and worse while the kid's eyes get larger and larger in surprise. What really pulls it into the real of reality comic strips avoided is that another strip shows the kid attending his uncle's funeral, and seeing the body all dressed up in the casket. The kid notes how phony everything is, how the body doesn't look like his uncle at all and wonders what they did to him. Finally the boy notes, "... and this music! He hated this kind of music!... it's sad...."

And then there was the taboo kids strips never dealt with until *Nuts*.

The parents who got into *real* arguments over *real* problems, such as when the father has a drinking problem.

One strip begins: "By far the most confusing thing about the rules made by the grown ups was that while they supposedly were for everybody, they were obviously just for kids and not for grown ups at all."

(Standing at the front door of a home as the family is leaving a party. The kid's parents are named Harry and Madge.)

HARRY: That wassa swell party! Really hadda swell time, Bess an' Harlan!

HARLAN: It was great havin u guys, Harry!

KID (thinking): I hate it when they get so weird!

(In the car.)

HARRY: Where's the keys? Oh yeah, here they are. Now where's the lock? Ha, ha, ha!

MADGE: You're sober enough to drive, aren't you, Harry?

HARRY: Whayamean, hon? Course I am.

KID (thinking): Oh, oh....

(A horrible squeal of brakes)

MADGE: Harry!!! For God's sake!

HARRY: Don't worry, I missed it!

KID (thinking bad words)

Later, another horrible noise.

KID (thinking): Jesus!!!

MADGE: Harry!

HARRY: Look Madge, it's my own damn curb! A man has a right to drive over his own... curb!

MADGE: Will you come around here and look what you did!!!

KID (thinking): They have absolutely no right to put me through this kind of crap!

A bit too intense for the Sunday funnies. Even with the language cleaned up, this would still have a hard time finding a place on the comics page in 1991 unless it were softened. After all, portraying parents in such a disturbing and unflattering light could be construed as being "anti-family."

In 1971, when this strip first began appearing, *National Lampoon* was one of the only places this feature could then appear in the national marketplace. This was at a time when the then-new phenomenon of underground comics were kicking down the restrictions on the form and the *National Lampoon* chose to reflect this in the variety of strips they ran in their funny pages section.

Wilson had become a fairly well known cartoonist by that time due to his work having appeared in *Playboy* for more than a decade and from reprint collections of his work which had been published. Gahan Wilson, unlike other *Playboy* cartoonists, didn't tailor his cartoons for the market but rather looked for markets which would publish his cartoons. His *Playboy* cartoons dealt with macabre subjects and ideas which were not risque in the least, just very strange. In the Sixties the slick publications which paid enough for a cartoonist to live on were looking for cartoons which were funny without being challenging in any way.

For *Playboy* just being funny was enough, and Wilson established himself there with two cartoons appearing in the magazine every month as well as an occasional feature. A 3-page feature by Wilson which appeared in *Help! #23* (March 1965) called *The Monster Craze* was not very different from the kind of work he also was drawing for *Playboy*. In fact in his reprint collections, it's impossible to differentiate by subject matter from the cartoons which appeared in *Playboy* and those which ran in other kinds of magazines. Wilson even had cartoons running regularly in *The Magazine of Fantasy & Science Fiction* for many years and this brought him fans who weren't familiar with his work in *Playboy*.

Even though the strange, offbeat one-panel cartoon, as perfected by Gary Larson, is popular today, its bizarre sense of humor has as its influence Gahan Wilson, among others, if not exclusively. Wilson even had a short-lived Sunday-only newspaper comic strip syndicated in 1974 and 1975 called *Gahan Wilson's Sunday Comics*. Unlike *Nuts*, which told a complete vignette in each installment, *Sunday Comics* was comprised of half a dozen unrelated cartoons grouped together under the single heading. In many respects they were the same sort of strange comics Gary Larson now does.

While other single cartoons of that time in newspapers were harmless slice-of-life gags, Gahan Wilson did cartoons with monsters or settings. One might be a scene in the future where a couple is watching a newsman on television weep uncontrollably as he reads the news, with the husband remarking, "Remember When They Didn't Cry?"

A selection of these were reprinted in *The Weird World of Gahan Wilson* (Tempo Books, 1975). While good cartoons, one has the feeling while reading them that Wilson had to soft-pedal his material to satisfy the needs of the newspaper syndicate as they lack the sharpness and the bite of much of the material found in his other collections.

Wilson's first collection was *Gahan Wilson 's Graveside Manner* (Ace Books, 1965) followed by *The Man in the Cannibal Pot* (Avon, 1970). Then his collections started being published in the larger, 8 1/2 x 11 trade paperback size with *I Paint What I See* (Fireside, 1971). This was followed in 1973 by *Playboy's Gahan Wilson* (*Playboy* Press) which ran 160 pages with half of them in full color. In 1978 came... *And Then We'll Get Him!* (Marek). In 1978 came another volume of *Playboy's Gahan Wilson* (Wideview Books). This was followed in 1979 by *Nuts* (Marek) which collected many, but not all, of this strip which ran in *National Lampoon* in the Seventies. Then in 1982 St. Martin's published *Is Nothing Sacred?*

As Wilson become more well-known, his work began appearing in publications as varied as *The New Yorker*, *Audubon*, *The New York Times Book Review*, *Esquire* and *Punch*. In the Eighties he was the film reviewer for the now defunct *Twilight Zone* magazine. He also now writes prose fiction in addition to being a cartoonist.

When *Nuts* ceased appearing in the late Seventies, it was somewhat abruptly and with a disturbing cliffhanger episode in which the kid gets sick and is being taken off in an ambulance. The last panel has the kid thinking about what could possibly happen next, and the caption ending the strip reads, "Next?" as though questioning why the kid is even expecting anything further to happen.

The 1979 reprint collection of *Nuts* does not reprint all of the strips (it was nearing the end of its run in *National Lampoon* at the time), but it does contain a number of pages of material entirely new to that collection. The prefix to the reprint collection bears the following touching message: DEDICATED TO ALL OF US.

THE QUIGMANS

They're ugly! They're weird! Too weird for some people, but they are definitely funny. "The Quigmans" may not be in as many newspapers yet as is "The Far Side", but with the recent publication by Harmony Books of the first collection of the single panel cartoon, it is acquiring an increasing following. No humor panel is more modern than this one.

All visuals this chapter © 1991 by The Los Angeles Times Syndicate

by James Van Hise

"Buddy Hickerson has been called an institution, but never a lending one. His emotions don't get mixed, his lighting is direct, and his septum never deviates. He uses obscenity only to save a life. He was born naked and has always been drawn to it. He has the look and feel of genuine hand-tooled leather. He seeks to unpeel the overdressed, underscore the overexposed, and overextend his welcome."

—From the jacket copy of THE QUIGMANS
(Harmony Books, 1990)

Since the success of Gary Larson's off-the-wall single panel cartoon "The Far Side", syndicates have been more open to unusual and singular styles of humor. Certainly one of the more singular is "The Quigmans". In fact, it was upon seeing "The Far Side" for the first time that Hickerson decided that there might be room in newspapers for his style of humor. His initial reaction to Gary Larson's strip was, "All right! Doors have been opened for the sick!"

The artist/writer who created "The Quigmans" is Buddy Hickerson, who attended North Texas State University as an art major. "I drew on the college newspaper," he explained, "which got me interested in the cartoon world. I did a lot of political stuff there but found out that the favorite thing I liked to do was just take the every day moments in life, because some of those were actually more rife for humor. Now I've swung back to liking to do political things, but it's hard to do that because of the lead time that I have. I have to send the cartoons in a month in advance. I've tried to get closer to the deadline, a la Doonesbury, but it's hard with my syndicate to do that. It's limited me on my political and more timely subjects.

"I did cartoons in college and then graduated in Dallas to work as a waiter," Hickerson continued with a grin. "I was also on the Texas Highway Department for awhile, scraping dead animals off the road, working with a really large man who had a really small head. I think he later subconsciously inspired the character Bob in my cartoons. Then I was at a party and I drew a caricature of somebody and he turned out to be an editor at the DENVER POST. He remembered me and called me up just at the point when I was about to starve. None of the waiter jobs suc-

ceeded—I was always getting fired. I even tried to work at Taco Bell and all this time I was doing my art at night. So at that point the editor called me and I got a job as a staff illustrator at the DENVER POST. That went on for a couple of years. After awhile I was forced to draw weather maps and things like that. On a couple occasions I put cities in the wrong places, kind of on purpose just out of rebellion because originally I was hired just to do illustrations. Then suddenly USA TODAY comes out with a lot of informational graphics and I was forced to do that against my will."

Buddy decided that the best way to get out of his uncomfortable job was to freelance.

"I'd always wanted to do a cartoon, but I thought that the family newspaper page was not the place for me. So I was doing things for NATIONAL LAMPOON and I realized suddenly that because of things like 'The Far Side' that newspapers were becoming a little more interesting. 'The Far Side' was the kind of humor I wanted to do because it was closer to the edge of bad taste."

So he drew up a batch of cartoons with no regular characters, which he originally called "Satire Lounge."

"There were about three syndicates that called about a week later. Two of them wanted me to do four-panel and one wanted

to stick to one panel if I could come up with some characters. So I came up with Bob, a large guy who is a victim of life in a way. He has a low self-esteem. Women dress him with their eyes at the beach and things like that. One cartoon that kind of sums it up is that when he's encumbered with a low self-image he takes a job as a speedbump. In fact that was the very first cartoon I drew, and it made me want to continue that character.

"Francine takes on the female roles in the cartoon, and finally there's Moe, who is a cruel guy. He doesn't appear very often. He used to appear more. And then there's Jowls, this sort of enigmatic dog who does not relish his role as pet for some reason. I think the Moe character (represented) the humor I did in NATIONAL LAMPOON (for a character) called Mr. Vengeance. In fact he even looked like the guy. That may be why Moe disappeared. Most of the stuff I came up for Moe to do would usually be censored."

Moe's evening was ruined when his date made it known that she too would like something to eat.

Buddy described some of the cartoons the syndicate felt went too far.

"He would be blowing squirrels away, I guess because one had bitten him as a child. Even if he was hitting somebody's shoulder or doing the smallest thing that wasn't the least bit offensive to me, the syndicate would receive letters. I guess because my characters are sort of menacing, anytime they did anything the least bit menacing—hit each other or throw something at each other—it would anger people with sensitive demeanors. That was why they started to limit me for awhile. I think now I could get away with more of that physically violent humor, which is the historical staple of all cartoons. That slapstick violence goes on in all cartoons on television. So I thought, why? What's the big deal? But I really think that it's because my characters are so ugly. They're not very cutely drawn and that shocks some of the more traditional comic readers."

His artistic interests reflect German expressionist painting and primitive art.

"I used to draw very realistically," Hickerson revealed. "I did portraits and that but I grew bored with rendering from life, which is one of the reasons my cartoon is kind of primitive looking, with a roughly hewn look to it. African art has influenced my cartooning, as has Picasso in the fine art realm. In illustration I've been influenced by Ralph Steadman, Mark Merrick (an artist out of New Jersey) and in the comics things like 'Krazy Kat.' Then there's a lot of underground artists, and more recently Larson. I like Bill Griffith's work a lot now.

"When I was a kid I read MAD magazine, then I became interested in a lot of European illustrators. The biggest influence would probably be Ralph Steadman. When I saw what he was able to get away with using distortion, I was really interested.

"It all comes down to what the editors allow to appear," Hickerson stated. "In my painting, in my fine art, I sometimes just play with forms and shapes. I might even take an old subject like The Rape Of The Sabine Women and make it my own by adding creatures and things. I just like to have fun with colors and shapes. You're always limited when you work commercially. It's a small revolt against that when I work in the parameters of a newspaper page. So I'm revolting against it, but at the same time I revel in it. It's a very strange desire, but I don't have the complete need to do fine art."

"The Quigmans" first appeared in March of 1985 and immediately sold to about fifty newspapers. From that beginning, the strip began to build slowly. The cartoons also appear on a series of greetings cards available from Paper Moon and Hallmark.

"A lot of papers have thought the cartoon too strange both looks-wise and humor-wise," Hickerson explained. "I've never had complaints about people not finding it funny, though. They find it interesting, but editors worry about the sector of the population that writes in alot. (The strip) stirs up all the crank writers. Luckily the papers we're in ignore that extreme element."

He admitted "The Quigmans" has been dropped by more papers than currently carry it.

"At one time I felt like no one liked my cartoon and I began to let it lag," he continued. "I did an entire month's worth of panels in a YMCA room in New York in a single night. Just me and a bottle of Muscatel, working on a bed with paper scattered everywhere and ink running all over me."

The popularity of the strip is great enough for the first collection of cartoons to be published in October with a second volume due late in 1991. "In fact, when the book came out I even went on a book tour," he said. "Random House, the owner of Harmony, sent me out to about five cities to sign books."

Hickerson describes his work habits as "a giant crunch at the end of the month," rather than drawing a little each day. "I still have that term paper mentality and I figure that I don't have to do it until the end of the month. That makes it seem like a chore, but I ultimately end up enjoying doing it. Actually it helps me to produce humor in that environment of fear. I find that I can force my brain to pop things out whereas if I'm sitting around and nothing is going wrong, it's hard to come out with humor.

"I am trying to fix that because that is strange and unhealthy. It's too much work in a period of three or four days. I do about twenty-four cartoons in about four days, actually. I write it when I can during the month, but I ultimately write most of it right there during those four days. So then I have the rest of the month to work on my painting and other stuff.

"I used to draw very realistically," Hickerson revealed. "I did portraits and that but I grew bored with rendering from life, which is one of the reasons my cartoon is kind of primitive looking, with a roughly hewn look to it."

"There's one pretty darn important fact that's occurred in the last three years," Hickerson hastened to add, "and that's the fact that I've taken on a co-writer. I took him on Mike Stanfill because of my other work. He used to write twenty-five percent of them, but now he's up to about fifty percent. So he's really one-half of the writing of the cartoon these days."

Looking over "The Quigmans", one would think it difficult for Buddy Hickerson to find a collaborator with the same skewed view of reality. The cartoonist explained that he's known Mike Stanfill since they were in college together.

"I've known the guy for ten years and it seems like he's always thought the same way as me, although he's a little bit more manic, and more neurotic. He's like me to an extreme. I think he's much more fertile. He's just got a natural gift for these ideas just coming out of his head. He's like a fountain of humor. He has a great mind for it and I find myself leaning on him more and more because I'm also doing other projects. In fact one of the projects I've got on the burner is a sitcom in a very early stage of development."

Buddy described his creative brainstorming sessions with Mike Stanfill by explaining, "We network on the ideas. We'll get on the phone and he'll add to an idea to mine and I'll add to an idea to his. Or sometimes we'll just say words. I'll say something like 'Takes leave of his senses,' and Mike will say that could be something like a guy walking away from his hands and arms and legs on a table. Then we'll say something like 'mushrooms' and we'll think of a mushroom cloud and think of a woman coming home from the grocery store and the caption ultimately is, 'Darn, I forgot to pick up some mushrooms.' So the whole neighborhood is going up in an atomic bomb and she's thinking about her groceries.

"It seems like more often than not Bob has negative qualities. I think that's basically the constant. It may be exposing all the failings I've had in my dating career. Francine probably represents all the women that have rejected me, too. Bob calls her up and she says, You called at a bad time, Bob—the Eighties, and I can't get married right now—it would lead to promiscuity. Things like that."

"It's a great way to work because it actually gets it done twice as fast. I know that there are some people who are upset that I have a collaborator now. I don't think the quality would be this good if I'd kept doing it alone for six years. I just had this idea that I was going to run out of steam.

"It happens to people who do something every day. It depends on what you're doing, and I don't know what it is about the type of work I do, but it's not natural for me to write, and I have to push myself to do it. So suddenly I find myself being a humorist when actually I started out as an artist—that's the natural work for me. It's a challenge, and I think that's the interesting thing about it that keeps you motivated."

Not all of the cartoons he turns in are found acceptable by the syndicate. Sometimes they feel Hickerson has gone too far with his humor.

"One was of The Absent-Minded Electric Knife Slayer," he recalled. "He's standing there saying, 'Lady, you got an extension cord?'

"There was also one about the discovery of the color wheel and it was a gay caveman who discovered the color wheel and he was sort of designing things.

"Then there was an Indian one. For awhile they were not letting me use phrases like, 'Me go on hill and watch Love Boat.' They wouldn't let me use that kind of language. I had to use average language for Indian talk.

"They actually sent me a list once of six things that were offensive that I couldn't do. There was excrement, ethnic humor, the handicapped and it went on from there."

In describing "The Quigmans", the cartoonist stated, "It's almost like an inward bound, over-attention to these trivial aspects of life. Bob seems to be somebody who is that way. He's somebody in love with the minor little things in life, and yet it's a bent perspective, too. I like the strange, surreal quality he conjures up."

One cartoon shows a woman standing holding what appears to be a hair-dryer while half of her head is blackened. The caption reads: "Francine, have you seen my flare gun?". This was a Mike Stanfill idea. Another shows Bob sitting under a tree with the caption: "Bob liked to sit and reminisce about all the good times other people had."

"It doesn't take a lot to fulfill Bob's life," Hickerson stated, describing that particular character in the cartoon. "Francine gets easily impressed by his little accomplishments, such as when he's in a bar and he's downing all these bottles and she says, *That's your sixth bottle, Bob. I always adore an Aqua Velva man.* In a way it's funny to say you want to say these things, but when you're doing a cartoon every day, you have to do other ideas too, and that can confuse the issue. It's not like doing a little film and having this perfect concept worked out.

"A cartoon is always going to change from the intentions to the concept. The concept I thought I had when I start a cartoon sometimes alters. Sometimes he's less of a loser. Sometimes he's a pathetic slime-mold. It almost seems like whatever suits the oddity of the moment.

"It seems like more often than not Bob has negative qualities. I think that's basically the constant. It may be exposing all the failings I've had in my dating career. Francine probably represents all the women that have rejected me, too. Bob calls her up and she says, *You called at a bad time, Bob—the Eighties,* and *I can't get married right now—it would lead to promiscuity.* Things like that."

Buddy Hickerson likes to play with his reader's mind. Even though "The Quigmans" has only existed for six years, he recently did a 25th anniversary installment of the strip.

"I acted like I'd been doing this for twenty-five years, and ran a cartoon that I claimed appeared in 1966. It was this 'Hi & Lois' style; a real dated Sixties look with some kind of caption about trying to go to Canada to evade the Draft. It actually fooled people. They didn't know the cartoon was that old. I said, 'Yeah, I started the cartoon when I was six years old!'

"I've decided that I'm going to do more like that: next month, the 200th anniversary, and finally end up doing the 2,000th anniversary with Egyptian costumes."

Hickerson said he loves the variety of humor used on comics pages today.

"The bigger variety the better, obviously," he noted. "Like I said before, it became the time to do a newspaper cartoon for me because of 'The Far Side' and 'Doonesbury' and all of these darker visions.

"And 'Zippy'! I never would have imagined an underground like 'Zippy' appearing as a daily cartoon in family newspapers.

"There are younger editors and people who realize there is an audience for that. It's happening everywhere. Stranger and more daring projects are getting done and that's encouraging. More and more of that is happening.

"The newspapers are well aware of their wide audience. It's not like television in that you're obviously going for a target audience. The newspaper comics page is everyone. They have to pay attention to how many per niche, and they think they know these niches, but some of them have the wrong idea.

"Many, many newspapers had the wrong idea. They consistently kept out the greater number of quality cartoons. I still see so many things that are lame, although in somebody else's opinion they're fine. People have a low expectation for humor, and have different ideas for humor. They like things like 'LuAnn,' which is just a dog and a little baby doing cute things which most humorists would just cast aside. They might think of them and see that this might lead to something else rather than just staying with that idea, but it's non-threatening."

Hickerson doesn't have a lot of use for "cute" strips such as "Garfield". As a parody, he did a panel with a cute dog and a caption which read: *Due to a slippage in the 'Quigmans' ratings, I'd like to introduce a NEW CHARACTER today. . . He's Cuddles, the irresistible puppy with big, moist eyes!* Buddy quickly found out why newspapers run comic strips of that variety.

"We've gotta get off this planet FAST! I've never felt so . . . USED!!"

"When I went to the bank, the women there were so happy that I was doing this character, and it was just a joke!" he recalled. "It was the first time this one girl even mentioned that she liked the cartoon."

I suggested he could always add Cuddles to the cast but have the dog do horrible things that looked cute. *(Editor's note: Which wouldn't be too different from the original, Garfield, come to think of it.)*

"I actually had a friend who was going to do a strip like that once," he said. "He couldn't get it syndicated. Someone was petrified of it for some reason. It was about a cute dog that went around terrorizing everyone. It was a great idea for a cartoon, but I guess people are afraid of doing something like that."

When "Mother Goose & Grimm"'s recurring motif of Grimm and toilets and fire hydrants arose, Hickerson remarked that Mike Peters can get away with things in his strip that Buddy's syndicate won't allow.

"I cannot do a dog with a fire hydrant, but he can, because he just does them!" he noted. "That's good that he does and the syndicate lets him, but mine's a little squeamish."

In summing up what he's doing with "The Quigmans," Hickerson stated, "I'm more into rebellion against the traditional comic form, hence the crude, childlike drawings. To me, it's just not worth doing the strip if I'm not creating something that is somehow new and different. When someone says, 'What is that? Is that a leg? Is that a cat or a dog?'—I love that! There's a lot of people out there who just don't understand it and who don't want it."

Special thanks to the Los Angeles Times Syndicate for arranging this interview with Buddy Hickerson.

"Many, many newspapers had the wrong idea. They consistently kept out the greater number of quality cartoons. I still see so many things that are lame, although in somebody else's opinion they're fine. People have a low expectation for humor, and have different ideas for humor. They like things like 'LuAnn,' which is just a dog and a little baby doing cute things which most humorists would just cast aside. They might think of them and see that this might lead to something else rather than just staying with that idea, but it's non-threatening."

TANK McNAMARA

Out of all the subjects ripe for humorous exploration, oddly enough sports, a subject familiar on very profound levels to many Americans, has received the briefest of attention in comic strips. Probably more Americans follow professional sports than own cats, but felines get more exposure on the comics page than professional sports does. Only Tank McNamara, written by Jeff Millar and drawn by Bill Hinds, has attempted to offset this, and it does so by bringing the lofty heights in which athletic competition is held more down to earth where it really lives.

by James Van Hise

Tank McNamara, the sometimes fumble-mouthed sportscaster who is the title character in the long-running strip by Jeff Millar and Bill Hinds, is an archetype. Not based on any one person, he is an amalgam of every sportscaster who ever got his job because he used to be a big name (or at least recognizable) professional athlete. While no single person served as the basis for Tank, there was one person who gave Jeff Millar the idea to create the character.

"I was watching a Tank-type struggling through the sports on a local newscast (not necessarily in Houston, where I live)," Millar recalls. "He fumble-mouthed through the baseball scores with marginal intelligibility; but when the poor guy came to the results of an important European car race, you could tell he was about ready to buy the farm. 'Jacky Ickx' nearly sent him into a labial arrhythmia; but the name of the race, which occurred last in the sentence, was the heart punch. Guess how he pronounced 'Grand Prix.' Yep."

That was in 1973. Even after Millar had worked out the main character and the type of strip it would be, he needed an artist.

"A couple of inquiries put me onto Bill Hinds. He was then 23, freshly graduated from Stephen F. Austin University in Nacogdoches, Texas, and was in the process of genteelly starving to death as a freelance cartoonist." Bill drew up six weeks of dailies and three Sunday strips that Millar had written. The first syndicate they showed it to was the Universal Press Syndicate because, as Millar puts it, "they would most likely be receptive to iconoclasm, satire and other impolite attitudes." He was right. *Tank McNamara* began its still uninterrupted run Aug. 5, 1974.

In describing his approach to the strip today, nearly 17 years later, Jeff Millar states, "I have two lives. In one I am the co-creator and writer of *Tank McNamara*, and in the other I'm the film critic and humor columnist of the *Houston Chronicle*. I had been writing about sports in a somewhat iconoclastic manner in my humor column,

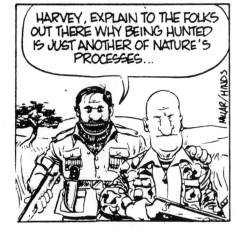

and I transferred that attitude to the comic strip. It's an attitude I've developed in my experiences since childhood. Athletics always brought more of a recognition and a reward than academics. I just thought that's the way life was until I got into my adult years."

In describing how he writes about sports in his column, Millar explains that he approaches it "in a kind of anti-chauvinistic manner. I write a different kind of column. I don't go about both the same way. I have sort of a cast of imaginary people and most of my thoughts about football are put in, as I said, sort of an anti-chauvinist way by using extensive statements made by people who hang out in a bar. My own personal class artists are lower middle class, blue collar. Those are my origins and hence those are the characters hanging out in the bar. They call them ice-houses down here.

"Those characters are alternate-me's, what I would have grown up to become but for a twist of fate here and there. And they speak with pride about their obsession with sports and their dedication to sports teams and their own sense of importance of sports. When you grow up in Texas, the ritual of football is terribly important, especially in small towns. I'm sure you've heard about the book *Saturday Night Lights*. I've only read about it, and sight unseen I can say that if it's not the truth on a page by page, statement by statement basis, the overall judgement is true because I grew up in that environment. I've seen the enormous emotional investment that residents of a small town make in their local high school athletic teams.

"First of all, until recently, and until the world had the ubiquitous television and satellite dishes, there wasn't a hell of a lot to do in small towns."

Yet Jeff Millar, a sports fan who grew up in a small Texas town, did not turn out the way the people he writes about did, and certainly not the way many of his contemporaries on the sports scene did. "I guess you go with what you're good at. Like every boy, I tried it. I was big for my age, I went to a small high school, and to please my father I went out for football in the 11th grade, and I discovered how low my pain threshold was. I was big for my age but I was clumsy; I didn't have any athletic ability. So I sought approval elsewhere. I sought it in academic and intellectual achievement, and got what everybody's after; some sort of stroke. So I got it, but I didn't get it in the quantities that an athlete does."

Millar did a variety of writing in high school and college before he began writing for newspapers.

"In high school I wrote plays. I was always interested in theater and am an amateur actor. I wrote one-act plays, skits for assemblies. Things like that. The class size was such that I couldn't work on the school newspaper, such as it was; it just two mimeographed sheets back then. It wasn't until I got to college that I worked on a newspaper."

Some years later Millar also wrote a novel, called *Private Sector*, a thriller published in 1979. "It's the kind you'd read at the beach or on an airplane," the author explains. "It was about a husband and wife, one's a journalist and the other an attorney, and by mutual decree they don't discuss what they're working on at home, and it turns out that each of them are working on the same thing but they don't know it, and that leads to some dangerous situations.

"The sales of it were disappointing, and because of that my agent wasn't able to sell my idea for a second one. Plus the trouble with writing a second novel is that now you know how much work it is. Had the first one been a roaring success and had a movie sale, I might have stayed with it, and I might still do another one some day. But my ideas for novels tend to be technology thrillers and my ideas get dated fast. *Private Sector* is quite dated right now."

Even though *Tank McNamara* appears on the sports page in 90 percent of the newspapers where it's run, by Millar's reckoning, it can nonetheless be read and enjoyed by people who have no serious interest in professional sports, but who are nevertheless amused by the excesses of the subject.

"I tried to make Tank understandable to people who weren't into sports," Millar states matter-of-factly.

Since Millar draws many of the ideas for the strip from stories in the headlines, I asked him whether he'd

"Those characters are alternate-me's, what I would have grown up to become but for a twist of fate here and there. And they speak with pride about their obsession with sports and their dedication to sports teams and their own sense of importance of sports."

be dealing with the recent incidents involving the banning of beer sales at sports events. He replied, "We've pretty much done that already. Generally we have found out that there is no shortage of ideas. Things happen in real life faster than we can think them up, and sometimes the ideas are standing in line and you can't always get around to all of them before they get old. So while I saw and noticed what is happening in Buffalo, the combination of the football season being almost over, and our lead time, and the fact that we've done this sort of thing before, argued against using this subject. But we may get around to it next year."

One subject the strip hasn't gotten around to is the event involving the World Wrestling Federation, which basically admitted that professional wrestling was phony in order to sidestep the safety guidelines that promoters of real sporting events are required to follow. Regarding the admission involved in this revelation, Millar responds that he didn't think that anyone ever really thought that pro wrestling was real anyway. "I think everyone sees it as sort of a passion play. But again, that got added to my list of things to do, but I haven't gotten around to it yet. I might still."

A recent oddball series in the strip involved football scouts going to a strange, out-of-the-way school called the Stephen King College in search of rookie football players. There the scouts found the team holding practice sessions in cemeteries and the like. Millar explains that this is just an example of the humor of hyperbole since scouts do go to backwoods colleges looking for unknown talent.

"I figure that whatever they put in the sports section is considered sports. Whatever Sports Illustrated writes about is considered sports. So I cover the waterfront in search for ideas."

"And also I like to mix things up, take things that are in the public eye and sort of arbitrarily jam them together. And the humorous extension of an obscure place, and someone going into a small town looking for jocks happens to run into a small town that Stephen King uses in his fiction. It's absurdist. It is, after all, a comic strip. I like to write bigger than life."

In discussing the kinds of cartoon art which influenced Millar himself in his early years, he explains that his grounding in humor was not so much in comic strips as in animated cartoons that he watched on television as a youth.

"When I think, in terms of cartoon art, what influenced me in terms of comic strips were the great Warner Brothers cartoons of the Forties and Fifties. I admire the people who created those very much, and my partner, Bill Hinds, teases me that I'm trying to write for animation rather than for static drawings. The style of humor. The timing; especially timing. You can do something like timing in a comic strip, but it's very hard."

Although Millar often depicts die-hard sports fans who have three or more televisions in order to watch multiple sports events and the like, such exaggerations (even when they're not exaggerations) are taken with good humor by his readers.

"People who are die-hard sports fans tend not to object to depictions of sports fans unless it's combined with something, some sort of criticism, real or implied, of something to which they've given their own allegiance. No one has ever objected to just the depiction of hard-core sports fans, at least not that has ever gotten back to me. However if you're a hard-core sports fan and your team is the San Diego Chargers and I make fun of the San Diego Chargers, then I'm going to hear about it."

As a rule Millar doesn't get a lot of mail from his readers.

"When I first got the comic strip I thought that I'd have to get a secretary to handle all the mail, but I get very little."

There are certain subjects he covers once in awhile which are guaranteed to pull mail, such as when he does a hunting scenario, one which usually involves the paramilitary character named Lance Savage.

"There's no (better) way to pull mail than to do something about hunting or guns. It's a guaranteed response. I do it every now and then just to make the sports editors aware that we're out there. It's the usual doctrinaire, knee-jerk reaction. The same key words show up."

When asked if he has ever done any strips that the syndicate didn't like or that editors didn't like, Millar states, "Yes, and it all depends on whose ox is being gored. It amazes me that people will take offense at something that wasn't intended to be offensive. For instance, if you do something that *appears* to poke fun at an ethnic community, the editors of newspapers where that ethnic community is large and influential, will arbitrarily scratch out that ethnic entity and substitute another ethnic entity where the population there is relatively small."

It has nothing to do with whether what Millar said was an accurate appraisal of a situation.

"I've asked an editor, 'Is this not true?' and he says, 'Yes, but that's not the point.' That's a direct quote. I was speechless when he said that. I've done things where I said, I hope this stirs things up; just to get people to talk about it and say, 'Did you see *Tank McNamara* this morning?' I think I lack something that truly effective political satirists have, which is my feeling for the jugular vein. I don't get off by offending people, but I think a really good satirist does get off by offending people.

"I certainly offend people inadvertently, but I know there are people out there reading it who are real people with real feelings and I don't like to make people feel bad without some justification. I like surgical strikes, as it were." At times his satire does zero in on specific ideas and targets. "When I feel it's justified, and I can precision bomb, then I go for it."

Although most people think of the traditional team sports when they think of the subject, Millar feels that the field is a wider one than that.

"I figure that whatever they put in the sports section is considered sports. Whatever *Sports Illustrated* writes about is considered sports. So I cover the waterfront in search for ideas. My personal feelings about hunting are fairly neutral. We often cast plagues on both houses. We also have poked fun at nut case environmentalists. We had this group who would throw themselves out of airplanes to draw a hunter's fire when they'd be shooting at ducks on the first day of hunting season.

"It's not safe to assume that because we do a strip about guns that we are anti-gun, just as it is not safe to assume that because we do a strip about hunters that we are

anti-hunters. People like Garry Trudeau do it. And some do it obliquely. We just do it somewhat less obliquely. I'm not sure that I have a lot of answers (on issues).

"I have questions and a comic strip is a good place to raise questions. It's not that good a place to supply answers, and I never felt myself really equipped to advise people on what sort of morals they should have. There are plenty of people out there who are fully equipped to do that."

Millar does have some very specific opinions about the world of professional and amateur athletics and he doesn't hesitate to include this world view in his strip. In fact it permeates most of the stories in the strip to a greater or lesser degree.

Says Millar, "Sports is fun and sports is entertainment, but it is not the molder of young men. People keep seeming to want to justify sports as having a value that is greater than entertainment. It's the maxim that the Battle of Waterloo was won on the playing fields of Eton carried to an absurdist extreme. That it's going to mold character and build the leaders of tomorrow by playing football.

"I find it doubly ironic that through no instigation of their own, young athletes are expected to be role models for children of both sexes. First of all, that's a very poor choice of role model because these young men are held up as examples at the time in their lives when they are guaranteed to make their most foolish mistakes. Males, or females too, in any profession, be it athletics or being a CPA, those years between 18 and 32 are when you do the dumbest things in your life! I don't care if you're a jock or a member of the U.S. House of Representatives. And yet they're expected to adhere to this fantasyland code of conduct so that the little kiddos out in Omaha will have a good example to follow, which is absurd."

Then there are major league sports wherein entire cities put a burden on the football or baseball team in that if the team is doing well, that makes the whole city look good. Although there have been examples of riots when a team has lost an important game, Millar feels this is rare and says, "That's the European model. Americans are somewhat less inclined to riot. They sometimes run amuck in defeat or in victory." Sometimes it's hard to tell the difference.

"I think a more subtle and pernicious effect is the internalization of victory," Millar explains. "Some people, ill advisedly, will make a large emotional investment in the outcome of sports events. They cast the participants in the sports events as their proxies running about as surrogates for them, and their own spirits rise and fall in direct proportion to them. It becomes a very serious business. It's ill-advised, let's put it that way. If you're going to make something your emotional surrogate, don't do it with a baseball team or a football team."

Yet while genuine tragic riots have occurred in Europe and South America at soccer matches, this sport has never managed to capture the popular American imagination the way that football and baseball has. Millar believes there's an interesting reason for that.

"I think Americans tend to view sports where you can't use your hands as somehow disenfranchising, suspicious and foreign. So that blows off soccer. I think they make the investments in baseball and football because that's where the media coverage is. Football especially, because it's held on the day of rituals, Sunday. So from that comes the ritualistic identification. As a rule I don't think about it in quite these pretentious terms. That just sort of occurred to me."

Although *Tank McNamara* is the only comic strip that Millar writes, he did develop another one which ran briefly in 1979.

"I started a second comic strip and it was a complete flop. In it, I attempted to do with the entertainment industry what I do with the sports industry in Tank. I was reading over some of them recently and realized why it deserved to fail. It only lasted a few months. The writing was weak."

Millar said there are so many ideas that sometimes they line up behind each other. When asked if there are times he feels the strip writes itself, he laughs and remarks, "I wish it would. But it's still the same old struggle to do straight line, punch line and cultural background in 80 words. The topics more or less present themselves, but it is still a struggle to make it work in a comic strip."

Since *Tank* mostly appears in the sports sections, Millar was asked whether this could give him an advantage in perhaps trying to get the strip to be run slightly larger since comic strips have been steadily shrunk by newspapers over the years.

"I guess Garry Trudeau did, but we've never felt we had the clout to make that happen. Anyone who does a comic strip would like to see it run larger. Actually the quality of the reproduction is what has gone down. The printing plates don't stand up to as many runs so the linework has to be bolder."

In describing the style of humor in comic strips today as opposed to the approaches in humor taken in the '50s and '60s, Millar has some interesting observations.

"There seems to be more overt social comment now than there was in the '50s and '60s in comics. This is not to say that the '60s, '70s and '80s brought overt social commentary to the comic pages for the first time. I'm not a scholar but I'm sure you realize that *Mutt & Jeff* was a social commentary strip when it began its life. Even *The Gumps* was. It just changed over time. So I wouldn't say that *Tank* is particularly new in that particular area, and it's certainly not one of the first of its kind."

Unlike many other comic strips whose reprint volumes crowd the shelves in book-stores, collections of classic *Tank McNamara* strips have been few and far between. In addition to a 1978 collection called *The Tank McNamara Chronicles*, there's only been one other volume, and it's long out of print.

"To my knowledge there are no other ones planned at this time," Millar reports. "The reprints don't sell too well, I think because it's so topical. *Tank McNamara*, unhappily for us, doesn't have much of an afterlife. It's as perishable as lettuce. I've tried to think of ways to counteract that, like putting out an annual or something; a *Tank McNamara* yearbook. But I haven't really found a way to get around it. So it's either that or people aren't interested in buying a *Tank McNamara* reprint under any circumstances."

When asked if there were specific things he wanted to accomplish with the strip when he created it, Millar replies, "I am not a strategic thinker. *Tank McNamara* enters my consciousness one day a week when I have to write copy for it, and then it leaves for days at a time. Looking back over almost 17 years, I don't think I intended it to do anything more than make a little pin money on the side and serve as an outlet for my attitudes. In most papers it's over there in the sports ghetto and it's an iconoclastic, cynical satirical strip."

Special thanks to Universal Press for arranging the interview with Jeff Millar.

TEENAGE MUTANT NINJA TURTLES

It began as a comic book in 1985 and through sheer weight of its own success has made the leap to the newspaper comic strip page—a highly coveted position. Yet this newspaper comic strip is merely the latest incarnation of what has become a bonafide cultural phenomenon.

by James Van Hise

The phenomenon had humble beginnings. It started as just two guys and their comic book. With the unlikely sounding title *Teenage Mutant Ninja Turtles*, writer/artists Kevin Eastman and Peter Laird had conceived, written and drawn a comic book they thought had merit. Based on their past experiences in having problems finding publishers who shared their artistic visions, they decided to publish it on their own.

"It was May '84 when we put out that first issue," Laird recalled during an interview in late 1986. "At that time we weren't even sure that we could sell those 3,000 copies of the first printing of the first issue." In late '86, issue #9 had just been published (it's now passed #34 and another title is published concurrently by Archie) and shipped 115,000 copies.

"I know that it sells more than some of Marvel's books. I've talked to some comic store owners who say that the number of *Turtles* they sell is comparable to the number of *X-Men* and *Teen Titans* (two popular titles from Marvel and D.C.) that they sell. I don't think that applies in every store in the direct market, but we've heard it from quite a few people."

The idea to go the self-publishing route with *Teenage Mutant Ninja Turtles* came about when another project they had submitted to some of the independent publishers received consistent rejections and they couldn't bear to see their latest brainchild go the same unhappy route.

"Our book *Fugitoid* was developed before we did the *Turtles*," Peter revealed. "We had 30 pages of it which we were sending around to all the independent publishers in the hopes of selling it as a backup story. However, all we got were all kinds of nice rejection letters. Then we came up with the idea of the *Turtles* and we couldn't bear the idea of rejection of it, so we decided to go with it ourselves. We really never thought of selling it to anybody else. It was something that we just felt strongly that we wanted to see in print and we knew that we could do it ourselves."

"It was all inspired by the self-publishing artists such as Dave Sim publishing *Cerebus* off on his own and having success with it," Kevin Eastman added. And so with seed money borrowed from relatives, they published the first issue of their comic book, and its sales enabled them to quickly repay the loan.

The *Turtles* began as a loving parody of writer/artist Frank Miller's work on *Daredevil* for Marvel Comics and *Ronin* for D.C., and in fact the cover of the first issue of the *Turtles* (at least in its early printings) is a takeoff on the style of the *Ronin* covers. The origin of the *Turtles* (which has been modified somewhat for the film

and later comic book renditions) is actually a spin on the origin of Marvel's *Daredevil* by adding one small sequence which Marvel Comics overlooked.

It has to do with a dislodged cylinder of radioactive material, a goldfish bowl containing 4 pet turtles and an open manhole where all wind up. The radioactive material mutates the turtles into humanoid forms down in the slimy depths of the sewer and they're discovered and trained by a similarly enhanced rat named Splinter. (In the *Daredevil* comic book, Frank Miller had introduced a character named Stick who had supposedly trained *Daredevil* years before.) In spite of an erroneous line in the newspaper strip referring to Splinter as having once been human, this is not true. Splinter was always a rat, just as Raphael, Leonardo, Michaelangelo and Donatello were always turtles.

Moving beyond the parody nature of the comic book's origin issue, it quickly developed an identity and sensibility all its own, even having a 4-issue storyline which was intergalactic in scope (the Mirage Press issues 4-7) while also revealing just what had been in that mysterious radioactive cylinder—and who it had belonged to.

The art on the comic book for its earliest issues was, like the writing, a successful collaboration of the talents of Kevin Eastman and Peter Laird. It was quite unique for comics as it took advantage of the black and white story format of their self-published comic book to make an abundant use of Craftint Doubletone. This is an attractive shading process used a great deal by the classic newspaper strip artists of the Thirties and Forties, and is all but a lost and abandoned art form today. Later color reprints of these issues, in the First Comics graphic novels, dropped much of the Craftint, but it remains in all the black and white reprints of these early stories.

"The duoshades was something that I'd played with a few times years ago," Laird stated. "I had some scraps of it lying around and Kevin saw it, tried it out and really liked it, so we decided to go for it."

"I thought it kind of went along with doing a parody of the origin of *Daredevil*," Kevin said, "since I was a Miller/Janson fan and Klaus Janson had done some really neat Craftint work on the actual *Daredevil* comic. He didn't use much of it, but what he did use really stood out. We thought it would be neat using the duoshade because we'd get a total of four different tones—black, white and two different shades of gray."

"It was all inspired by the self-publishing artists such as Dave Sim publishing Cerebus off on his own and having success with it," Kevin Eastman added. And so with seed money borrowed from relatives, they published the first issue of their comic book, and its sales enabled them to quickly repay the loan.

Prior to embarking on their creative self-publishing endeavors, Peter had been a freelance illustrator for 8 years, primarily doing editorial illustrations for a newspaper in Northampton, Mass. Kevin had done comics work for some New Wave comics published by Clay Geerdes and for Brad Foster's *Goodies* magazine.

While the initial groundswell of enthusiasm for the *Turtles* took the creators by surprise, they feel that they

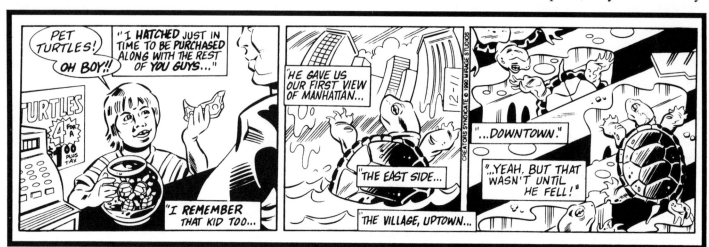

know why the book has a continuing following, although it involves a number of factors.

"There's a lot of action and the characters of the *Turtles* are appealing because they're basically nice guys," Laird stated.

"I think that it's because it's easy to read and has an interesting storyline," Kevin added. "We try to approach each book to contain the basic elements of adventure and excitement that you find in *Raiders of the Lost Ark*."

"We also try to keep the story-telling simple and direct," Laird continued, "and try not to get very convoluted with plots where many different things are happening simultaneously. We like to keep things pretty streamlined."

"Kevin and I have said to each other many times that we're trying to keep it, at most, PG rated, and it's worked out for the best since quite a large proportion of our audience are kids and we try to keep it at a level that's enjoyable for them. You can tell a good story without resorting to a lot of profanity or excessive violence, not that we don't appreciate that stuff in the material we like to read. There's a lot of violent action in our books, but not really very much violence. I think Kevin and I both see the difference between action and violence."

When readers of the comic books started pointing out that the turtles all seemed to look alike and that they could only be distinguished one from the other by the weapons they carried, Eastman and Laird decided that they wanted to do some stories which clearly defined the different personalities of the quartet. The result, the micro-series!

"We decided we wanted to do some kind of parody of the 4-issue mini-series and 12 issue maxi-series books," Laird related. "So we decided on the one issue micro-series. In those books we planned to go into the actual personality of each turtle a little deeper. Raphael was more of a berserker and is the rougher of them, so the *Raphael* book is really violent with a lot of action going on.

"*Michaelangelo* was the next one. We consider him the more fun loving—the joker of the crowd. So although his story was adventure, it was centered around toys and toy stores, with Michaelangelo playing in the snow and it's a little more light-hearted. Then there was *Donatello* and that was followed in December 1986 by *Leonardo*." They had considered additional micro-series, including one each on Splinter and Casey Jones, but these were never done.

Other *Turtle* related products (a role-playing game, tie-in comics on martial arts and how-to-draw the *Turtles*) were among the first licensed properties. These were drawn by other hands to free Eastman and Laird to draw the regular books they wanted to continue publishing. For a time they even published a companion title, *Tales of the Teenage Mutant Ninja Turtles* which lasted seven issues. This was dropped in favor of doing the regular title more often. Later they also licensed a separate series of *Turtles* comics to the Archie Comics Group which is aimed at younger readers and is more reflective of the approach taken in the animated cartoon series seen on television.

Regarding the full color reprints published in graphic novel form by First Comics (and of which four volumes appeared), Laird explained their artistic involvement with them when he described what they did on the first of the four volumes.

"Kevin and I went through and used some whiteout and some ink and touched up some faces and anatomy here and there. Plus, it's all been re-lettered. The first three issues were lettered by Kevin, but our current letterer, Steven Levine, has gone over it and re-lettered it." Plus 12 completely new pages appear in the first color volume in the form of two six-page stories.

"It was an experiment in that it was the first time that Kevin and I had done *Turtle* stories by ourselves. We each took six pages and did whatever we wanted to. Kevin's story was inked by Brian Brown. My story was inked by Jim Lawson."

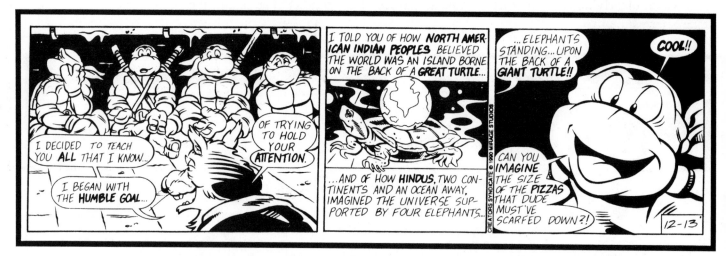

Over the years, the interest in the *Turtles* grew as the animated cartoon and the Archie Comic series brought new fans into the fold. A series of toys came next and 1990 saw the first motion picture. Lots of toys and tie-ins later, December 1990 saw the debut of a syndicated *Teenage Mutant Ninja Turtles* daily newspaper strip. Produced by Mirage Studios, the strip bears the Eastman & Laird byline next to the title, but the art is signed by various people, such as Clarrain, Brown and Berger on the Saturday daily strip each week.

The daily strip bears a closer relation to the Archie Comics version than it does to the original Mirage Studios publication. Interestingly, the strip manages to maintain a balance of humor and action and moves the story along at a much swifter pace than other more serious newspaper adventure strips like 'Spider-Man' and 'Batman.'

The *Teenage Mutant Ninja Turtles* newspaper strip was doubtlessly conceived due to the success of the 1990 film, which grossed $150 million and sold 8 million copies of the home video version. With the 1991 feature film following one year after the first film, the marketing of this successful enterprise shows no signs of slowing down.

When asked for advice to give up and coming cartoonists, Peter Laird stated, "Read widely, talk to lots of people and draw or write incessantly, and just practice. Hone your craft. And expect to be rejected before you get accepted."

"And protect yourselves," Eastman added, "protect your characters in the legal sense. And practice! Practice how to arrange stories. Study your favorite artists; pay attention not only to human anatomy but to the world that makes up the background, and draw everything!"

What Kevin Eastman and Peter Laird have proven is that if you come up with an entertaining idea and you have the talent to bring it off, the world really will beat a path to your door.

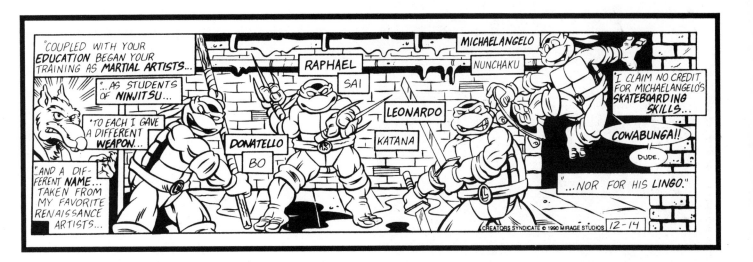

What Kevin Eastman and Peter Laird have proven is that if you come up with an entertaining idea and you have the talent to bring it off, the world really will beat a path to your door.

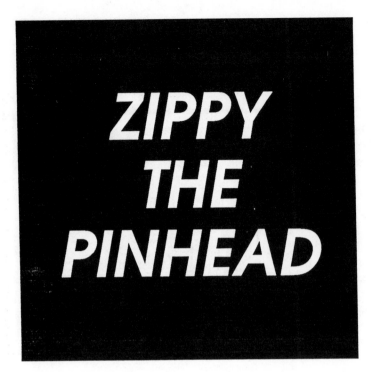

ZIPPY THE PINHEAD

From the underground comics of the Seventies to the comics pages of the Nineties, Zippy has managed to make the transition unfettered and unscathed. One of the most unusual comic strips in newspapers today, it is also one of the best written.

by Dan Whitworth

MBill Griffith's *Zippy*, currently syndicated in 200 papers nationwide, consistently manages to leap off the comics page and grab readers by the forebrain. Surrounded by cute babies and fat cats, yuppie-oriented strips and other banalities, he is a force for positive consternation. His yellow and red clown suit seems bright in the company of his neighbors, even on the black-and-white daily pages, and his responses to consensus reality (no longer the constant it used to seem) may be our only guide to survival in the post-post-modern world. It should come as no surprise that this genial but disturbing intruder comes from another world: he is the first character to reach the daily comics from the underground comics of the 1970s.

Griffith gained prominence in the undergrounds with such comics as *Young Lust*, *Tales of the Toad*, and *Griffith Observatory*. His sharp satirical sense, marked by a certain anger in his earlier years, earned him a loyal following. Mr. The Toad, his main character before Zippy, acted as a sometimes restricting focus for that anger, while the *Observatory* served as a forum for his more explicit social criticisms. Compromise, certainly, is not a trait associated with the soft-spoken cartoonist. Reach by phone at his San Francisco studio, he expressed his feelings about his work both today and back in the underground.

"It was a time when things were fairly political," Griffith recalled, "even when they weren't intentionally so. Even if you were just doing something surreal, or just thought you were telling a story, you were being political just by the very nature of the times and the people that were reading your work, since you were doing things that were 'alternative' and supplying an audience that was turned off to mainstream entertainment. Just by that very nature you were being political.

"My early approach isn't that different from the way I approach it now, which is to do comics out of a personal necessity feeling, as opposed to looking for a prime demographic spread. I'm not trying to please everybody and I'm perfectly happy that that's the way it is. Nobody wants to have a small audience, but I'm satisfied with the growth over the years.

"The feeling I have when I sit down to the drawing table isn't that different than it was in 1970, although at that point I think I and a lot of other people were a little looser, maybe, and I was struggling with how to be a cartoonist, too. It's one of those cases where, when you come from the underground, you have the luxury of learning your trade while you do it, with very little pressure on you to be any certain way or fulfill anybody else's needs. It was very free, but it was a real testing ground. A lot of cartoonists didn't keep it up. A lot of them were very good and then quit," Griffith observed.

"I really am grateful that I was part of it because it gave me a chance to become a cartoonist and see my stuff in print pretty quickly."

When asked about influences on his cartooning, Griffith recalled his childhood interests.

"I was really a comics fan as a kid, but only a very certain type of comics. Just *Mad*, the early *Mad*, and *Little Lulu*, *Scrooge*, *Superman* a little; in general, superheroes never interested me. Plastic Man was a big thing for me, which was, of course, a parody of superheroes. So my early influences to be a cartoonist, talking about the ages of 7 to 12, were mostly *Mad* and Jimmy Hatwell's *They'll Do It Every Time*. My *Griffith Observatory* springs from two influences: one, *They'll Do It Every Time*, and the other one is a strip that didn't have a title, but it ran weekly on Sunday. The cartoonist's name was W.E. Hill. The title changed each week. It was a full page.

"He would pick a subject and make observations on that subject. He did one called *Jazz Babies*, which were like jazz groupies. He went from the late teens to 1960. He is completely and utterly forgotten. He was a great cartoonist, in my opinion. He didn't do narratives, he didn't have a character, so that's why he's not remembered, probably. But Hill and Jimmy Hatwell were big influences on me."

Griffith did not, however, take a direct path to realizing his childhood ambition to be a cartoonist. A diversion, perhaps vital to his future development, arose as he grew older.

"I thought comics were something that you stopped reading when you got to be whatever I was, 14 or 15, and my thoughts turned more toward fine art. I think that was largely because of living next door to a fairly well-known science fiction illustrator by the name of Ed Emshwiller, who signed his work *Emsh*. He went through this transformation at exactly that time. I think he was always voted number one, got awards for being the best science fiction artist, and then, some time in the late Fifties, he began to sort of go beatnik.

"This is in Levittown, Long Island, which is the center of squareness of the planet, where everybody is living the exact same life, and here I was living next to the only beatnik in Levittown. I started getting interested in what he was interested in. He and my mother; my mother was sort of a crazy lady, and they exposed me to abstract painting, and the history of painting in general."

Emshwiller, a family friend, also gained fame as a pioneer of video art.

"I tried to be a painter from about '63 to '69, around there, in New York, with not much great success. Just an occasional show. But I think I was suppressing. In fact I know I was suppressing, this wise guy inside. So he came out, asserted himself again, in about 1969, and I started doing comics."

"I actually helped him do his early films. Before he became a video artist, he was a fairly well-known experimental filmmaker, from 1960 to whenever he started video. I would go out on location with him.

"I remember we went to visit a hermit who collected bottle caps," Griffith continued, "and he made his house out of bottle caps. I would just help him do things. He exposed me to a lot of art with a capital 'A,' even though commercial art was his background. I think he had a dual influence on me."

Ed Emshwiller majored in painting and illustration at the University of Michigan in the late Forties, and started doing science fiction illustration professionally in 1951 when he began working for *Galaxy* magazine. During the following 13 years he did more than 400 covers for books and magazines as well as hundreds of black and white interior illustrations for the SF magazines. He was nominated for the Hugo Award eight times and won five of those—1953, 1960, 1961, 1962 and 1964. In 1962 he made the short film *Thanatopsis* and on the strength of this he received a grant in 1964 to make the short film *Relativity* and a government commission to film *Faces of America*.

He took what he thought would be a one-year hiatus from illustrating but never returned. Although he did occasional illustrations for friends, he continued making such experimental films as *Three Dancers* and *Totem*. In 1971 he moved from film into the then-new field of videotape. Over the years he taught at such schools as Cornell, Yale and U.C. Berkeley. Emshwiller died July 27, 1990 at 65, but his short films are still popular at film festivals even though some were made more than 20 years ago.

Griffith studied art for several years at the Pratt Institute in Brooklyn, but except for a trip to Europe financed with his student loan, his efforts in the art world were not profitable.

"I tried to be a painter from about '63 to '69, around there, in New York, with not much great success. Just an occasional show. But I think I was suppressing. In fact I *know* I was suppressing, this wise guy inside. So he came out, asserted himself again, in about 1969, and I started doing comics.

"I didn't notice underground comics until they'd been going about a year. I started to see the early *Zap*'s and the early stuff in the *East Village Other* in New York, which was the main underground paper. I saw Crumb's stuff, and I noticed that a guy I went to art school with, Kim Deitch, was appearing in the *East Village Other*. I went down there to say hello to him and he encouraged me to be a cartoonist. I just did something, it was published, and that was the end of my painting. Overnight I realized, hey, 10,000 people are going to read this thing, and six people see my paintings. I think I'll try this."

Griffith fell in with Justin Green, Jay Kinney and other luminaries of the East Coast underground. Between 1969 and '72, the majority of these artists, including Griffith, moved to San Francisco.

"Everybody that was in New York came out here," Griffith explained, "because the New York underground comics scene was focused completely around the *East Village Other*, which spawned

something called *The Gothic Blimp Works*, which went through 10 issues or so. It took that long for the distributors, who were pretty much Mafia-controlled, to realize that it wasn't going to make them any money because it didn't have porno ads. It was just comics. The *East Village Other* made money, like the *Berkeley Barb* and all the other early undergrounds, because it was filled with "personal" ads, as they called them. When they realized we weren't going to make them any money, they stopped distributing it, so there was no reason to stay in New York any more."

"San Francisco, of course, was Mecca for cartoonists, because that was where all the publishers were. For a while there you could do anything and sell 20,000 copies."

In this environment, Griffith's work continued in earnest. In 1970, he met another New York expatriate, Art Spiegelman, with whom he would collaborate on one of the high points of the underground, *Arcade*, published from 1974 to 1975. Hoping to bring their fellow cartoonists to a wider audience, the two editors encouraged their contributors to do their best work. Although its seven issues had limited success in the general marketplace, *Arcade* featured consistently superb material.

Artists such as Robert Crumb, Aline Kominsky and Spiegelman produced very personal, frequently intense narratives. Spain Rodriguez' historical pieces and S. Clay Wilson's bizarre, lurid fantasies were also featured. Griffith's future wife, Diane Noomin, contributed stories of her character Didi Glitz, while Griffith himself produced strips on a variety of subjects. One such strip was a biography of the French painter Henri Rousseau, whose strange naivete at times seems to parallel that of Zippy; Rousseau's story was narrated by the playwright Alfred Jarry, one of literature's strangest characters, who sometimes appears in the Zippy strip even today. Zippy himself wandered the pages of *Arcade*, and with good reason: he had come to occupy more and more of his creator's attention.

"He first came to me as the result of an assignment," Griffith explains. In 1970, his friend Roger Brand was editing a comic entitled *Real Pulp Comics*, and asked Griffith for a contribution. "*Young Lust #1* had just come out, and he wanted me to do something in that vein, but make it stranger, he said; not about normal people. So I took him literally. Another friend of mine had a whole pile of photographs of sideshow freaks who apparently all lived, during the winter months when sideshows still existed, in this one town in Florida outside of Orlando. They sold pictures of themselves, and he had them all.

"I went through them, and there was a whole bunch of pictures of a pinhead by the name of Slitzy, who was a female, and was the pinhead that had the starring role of the three pinheads in the movie *Freaks*. She was still alive, as of the late Sixties, and selling pictures of herself. I saw these pictures and then remembered, oh yeah, I saw *Freaks* back in college in 1962. Those two things kind of collided in my head, and I thought, well, I'll do a story about a pinhead, and I'll make it a triangle. I called it *I Fell For A Pinhead But He Made A Fool Out Of Me*.

"That's where Zippy was born, although he only becomes Zippy toward the end of the strip. He starts out with another name. He's based on Slitzy, but I made him a male. At the time I didn't know Slitzy wasn't a male. That was the first appearance, and it was intended strictly, if I had any intentions at all, as a one-shot. I didn't have any thoughts of keeping the character going.

"But a few months later," Griffith continued, "working on *Tales of Toad #2*, or doing some Mr. Toad strips, I was already getting weary of Mr. Toad's hostility. He didn't modulate that much. He was a good character for me, but he didn't have that wide a range. I thought, why don't I do this Zippy character and put him in as a sidekick? Just have him come in there for one story and see what happens... and that was the way it started. Zippy was Mr. Toad's patsy for a number of stories, and then, little by little, the roles were reversed and Mr. Toad became Zippy's sidekick.

"I guess that reflected a change in direction in what I wanted to do with comics, as well as this quality of creating characters who then tell you what to do. Of course, that's a common thing among cartoonists. They'll tell you that a lot, that you create a character and, assuming the character has some blood in him, he will eventually start yanking your chain, instead of the other way around. By '74 or '75, he was what I was concentrating on, although I would do other things. And then in 1976, which was the next Zippy plateau, was when I started doing it as a weekly strip for the *Berkeley Barb*.

"More or less at the same time, the Rip Off Press, one of the underground publishers up here, started the Rip Off Syndicate, which lasted from '76 to '80, I believe. They took it and put it in more papers than just the *Berkeley Barb*. It was in about 25 or 30 weekly, alternative papers. In '80, Rip Off decided that their syndicate wasn't making them enough money, so they stopped doing it.

"I got the list (of papers) and I started doing it myself. Like Matt Groening after me, and a number of other people, I created a little one-man syndicate," Griffith stated.

"That's where Zippy was born, although he only becomes Zippy toward the end of the strip. He starts out with another name. He's based on Slitzy, but I made him a male. At the time I didn't know Slitzy wasn't a male. That was the first appearance, and it was intended strictly, if I had any intentions at all, as a one-shot. "

"In 1985, the *San Francisco Examiner* was taken over by Will Hearst (William Randolph Hearst III), who had some background in alternative publishing. He's the heir to the Hearst fortune, but he also was a young guy who came up somewhat influenced by the counter-culture years. He was aware of my work, I guess, 'cause he had his editor give me a call. I went down to the *Examiner*, and I assumed they wanted my weekly. They also had called Crumb, and this was when they hired Hunter Thompson, and a number of other people like that, that they were going to spice up their paper with.

"Like I said, I assumed he meant it as a weekly, and he said, 'No, I mean it as a daily.' I sort of did a double-take and said that I'd have to think about that one. Then I came back and I said, okay, if you pay me X amount of dollars... I made a bold move, just because I was sure he'd say no. And he agreed, and there I was."

Griffith began producing five strips a week for Hearst, and soon expanded to six. After a year at the *Examiner*, he was contacted by King Features, another Hearst company, who offered him a syndication deal.

"Once again my response was skeptical. My meeting with them was odd, because I basically gave them a list of demands, almost like I was taking hostages. I expected them to turn me down. I said I wanted to keep my copyright, I wanted the strip to be printed taller than the other strips, and I also asked for a certain amount of money that was a guarantee; I didn't want to take a chance. I said, why should I go from the *Examiner*, where they're giving me a nice little salary for the first time in my life, and go with you and take a chance and maybe just have five papers and never make a penny.

"After a certain advance, nothing excessive, but what I thought was a decent amount of money, they agreed to that, and they agreed to a very favorable merchandising split because I had a lot of merchandising already. All kinds of little things that I never expected them to agree to. Once they agreed to them, I had no choice. Having made my little move, I had to say 'okay.' In May of '86, it started being syndicated around the country by King."

The move to national syndication did not pose Griffith any real problems, as far as content was concerned.

"All during the underground comics days, the amount of references that I made specifically to drugs could be counted on two hands. It wasn't a big deal for me. I did work for *High Times* magazine, and I would do things like get Zippy involved in a drug smuggling story. *Young Lust* was full of raunchy sex, but those areas were not ever my main focus.

"By the time King Features or the *San Francisco Examiner* approached me, I didn't feel any compromise at all. In fact, I think it's kind of fun to be in a place like King Features where you can test their limits. They know I'm weird, and they like it. They think of me as the house weirdo, so I have certain advantages. I can introduce certain things there that a less conservative syndicate might not appreciate. At King Features, they know I'm weird and they expect it."

Griffith said that King Features only objected to one strip in the past five years. "I once did a strip in which I had Zippy read the list of ingredients in a Big Mac. At that time, McDonalds was placing little pamphlets in their stores claiming that their food was healthy; that it was just as healthy as a whole wheat sandwich with tofu, or whatever. They had printed all the ingredients and some of them, of course, were pretty odd sounding and artificial.

"I had Zippy read them as if it was a poem. He thought he had to read this in order to get a hamburger, so he got up in the line at McDonalds and spouted this to the server. I literally used the ingredients from this pamphlet. I didn't make anything up. But King said that McDonalds would undoubtedly write them and complain. I

did put that into one of my books, so it is out there. Since it was the first and only time they've ever done that, I let them get away with it.

"They have called me a few times in the past few years and said, 'This strip will offend so-and-so; we're going to get letters,' and I just tell them, sorry, you gotta' run it, and they do. They just called me a few months ago about something... I used (a) word... and they said, 'Can you change it?' I said no. They said, 'Aw, gee, I wish you would,' and I said no, I won't. Their solution to that was to send out a letter with each of those strips warning the editor, so they wouldn't just put it in their paper without knowing it was in there. No one didn't print it.

"They think of me as the house weirdo," Griffith reiterates, "and they know I'm going to do odd things, and it's not that they don't get nervous about it. They do. But they like that I do it."

Throughout his career, Griffith himself has appeared in his cartoons as "Griffy," who seems quite at ease with Zippy. The question arises: does Griffith have a personal relationship with Zippy?

"Oh yeah," he admits. "He's kind of a muse." Zippy even appears to Griffith in his dreams. "Although never as a drawn cartoon character. I always dream about him as a real person. He's pretty benevolent. He's a little frightening, sometimes. Zippy's the kind of character that, were he alive, and he approached you on the street, exactly the way he looks in my strip, spouting non-sequiturs and looking like he was enjoying himself tremendously, you would be amused and frightened at the same time, I think. A little more frightened, at first, or wary, at least. That happens, to a degree, when I sit down to do my strip; I have this little dialogue, and he sort of tells me what to do, and then I have to interpret it; translate it a little bit.

"In a weird way, maybe this society is ready for Zippy, because in some ways people have become more like Zippy over the years."

"He's somewhere in my brain, and I'm very conscious of the fact that it has to filter through all the parts of my brain before it can be put on the paper, because if it just goes out raw, which I used to do years ago, it has an unsettling, and sometimes even boring, effect on people. If Zippy literally were to do nothing but spout non-sequiturs, I don't think anybody would read him for very long."

So Bill Griffith screens the surreal intellect of Zippy through his own sensibilities to produce an understandable amalgam.

"I use some of his personality quirks and qualities to produce satire. So Zippy becomes Zippy and Griffy. They become a dual mechanism for my satirical impulses. Without Griffy, Zippy would be too much to take. My left brain and my right brain meet on the drawing board.

"Until Griffy became a permanent fixture in the strip, which happened years ago in the weeklies, I wasn't fully in control of my creation, because Zippy can be overpowering, and too crazy. By putting myself into it, and giving myself an extreme character... in my strip I'm cranky and more opinionated and more rigid than I really am, but by exaggerating those qualities I think the two characters bounce off each other in a way that produces a good relationship."

Griffith is still hoping to see Zippy reach more people through the medium of film. First optioned seven years ago, the Zippy movie has been through nine screenplay drafts so far. "It refuses to be made, and refuses to die," he observes. Randy Quaid has been picked to star, and a director has been set, but the project has yet to reach production. The distributor has pledged half of the budget, but the other half has yet to materialize. Numerous studios have been interested, but various factors, not the least of them the strangeness of Zippy, have proven to be stumbling blocks.

"Part of the reason it hasn't happened, I'm sure, is because I've been very much in control of the creative part of it, and insisted on that. Nobody can write or rewrite the screenplay but myself and my wife, Diane Noomin, who is also a cartoonist. We've written all the drafts; the last draft we did write with the director, so he helped, but he didn't actually write literally, the words. We had meetings and worked things out with him.

"That's how I want it to be. I want it to be a real collaboration. I know it's not a one-man, one-woman field. You have to collaborate with people. I don't want to be ashamed of the movie when it comes out. I don't want to sit in the front row and wince, and leave rich and embarrassed. I'd rather make less money and like the movie. I think I've probably held it up myself, somewhat, by insisting on having control over script and actors and directors."

The prospect of Zippy becoming a blockbuster hit doesn't seem too likely to Griffith; he'd be content with a cult success. Still, the movie might lead to unexpected results.

"In a weird way, maybe this society is ready for Zippy, because in some ways people have become more like Zippy over the years. With this remote control device that we're all clicking all day, I think the attention span of the average American is about as long as a commercial, which is about what Zippy is.

"Facetiously, but maybe with a grain of truth, I assume that some of the success that I've had in daily newspapers must be partly due to the fact that my audience has actually begun to catch up with Zippy's way of thinking. That's a frightening yet exciting thought.

"I suppose that if the movie comes out at the exact right time, maybe Zippy and America would meet at the same moment, and both understand each other completely, having never been introduced before."

Special thanks to King Features for arranging the interview with Bill Griffith.

FUNNY
STUFF

FURTHER READING

FUNNY
STUFF

MAGAZINES

Send a self-addressed stamped envelope for additional information and current prices.

AMAZING HEROES

Fantagraphics Books, Inc.

7563 Lake City Way

Seattle, WA 98115

COMICS INTERVIEW

Fictioneer Books Ltd.

234 Fifth Ave, Suite 301

New York, N.Y. 10001

COMIC RELIEF MAGAZINE

P.O. Box 6606

Eureka, CA 95502

COMICS REVUE

Fictioneer Books, Ltd.

234 Fifth Ave, Suite 301

New York, N.Y. 10001

THE COMICS JOURNAL: THE MAGAZINE OF NEWS & CRITICISM

7563 Lake City Way N.E.

Seattle, WA 98115

FUNNY TIMES: A MONTHLY HUMOR REVIEW

P.O. Box 18530

Cleveland Heights, Ohio 44118

BIBLIOGRAPHY

BLOOM COUNTY

Comics Interview #6 (Aug. 1983): "Writer/Artist Berke Breathed," interview by Jim Massara.

The Comics Journal #125 (Oct. 1988): "Can Breathed Be Taken Seriously?", an interview by Mark Jannot.

The Comics Journal #127 (Feb. 1989): "An Interview With Bill Watterson"

Classics of Western Literature (*Bloom County 1986-1989*): "Final Word" by Berke Breathed.

The Encyclopedia of American Comics: *from 1987 to the Present*, Edited by Ron Goulart (Facts On File books, 1990)

Time (Dec. 25, 1989): "A Hooligan Who Wields a Pen," an interview with Berke Breathed by Daniel S. Levy

CALVIN & HOBBES

Calvin and Hobbes(1987)—collection published by Andrews, McMeel & Parker.

The Comics Journal #127 (Feb. 1989)—Interview: Bill Watterson conducted by Richard Samuel West.

Entertainment Weekly (Oct. 5, 1990)—"Black & White & Read All Over" by Ken Tucker.

The Essential Calvin and Hobbes(1988)—collection published by Andrews and McMeel.

Honk! #2 (1986)—An interview with Bill Watterson by Andrew Christie.

DOONESBURY

Collage #19 (July 1971)— "An Interview With Garry Trudeau" by Jay Maeder

The Doonesbury Chronicles (Holt, Rinehart and Winston, 1975)

Newsweek (Oct. 15, 1990)—"Real Life With Garry Trudeau" by Jonathan Alter

The People's Doonesbury (Holt, Rinehart and Winston, 1981)

The San Diego Union (Dec. 17, 1990)

Time (Feb. 9, 1976)— "*Doonesbury* : Drawing and Quartering for Fun and Profit"

THE FAR SIDE

The Far Side Gallery by Gary Larson (Andrews & McMeel, 1984)

The Far Side Gallery 2 by Gary Larson (Andrews & McMeel), 1986

Forbes (Dec. 12, 1988): "Faces Behind the Figures—Funny money" by Steve Weiner

People (Feb. 4, 1985): "Loony 'Toonist Gary Larson Takes Millions For A Daily Walk On *The Far Side* " Written by Fred Bernstein, reported by Mary A. Pradt

The Pre-History of The Far Side : a 10th Anniversary Exhibit by Gary Larson (Andrews & McMeel, 1989)

Rolling Stone (Sept. 24, 1987): "Creatures from the Black Cartoon" by Peter Richmond

GARFIELD

Comics Scene #5 (1988): "Catching *Garfield* By The Tale" by Bob Miller

Comics Interview #6 (Aug. 1983): Berke Breathed interviewed by Jim Massara

The Encyclopedia of American Comics: From 1897 to the Present (Facts On File books, 1990) Edited by Ron Goulart

Entertainment Weekly (Oct. 5, 1990): "Black & White & Read All Over" by Ken Tucker

Great Comic Cats (Troubador Press, 1981) by Bill Blackbeard and Malcolm Whyte

National Geographic World (Dec. 1985): "The Man Behind The Cat"

New York Times Book Review (July 27, 1980): "Behind The Best Sellers—Battle of the Cats" by Edwin McDowell

People (Nov. 1, 1982): "*Garfield* Goes Hollywood—With Jim Davis On His Cattails—For Feline Fame And Fortune" by Mary Vespa

Saturday Evening Post (Nov. 1984): "Jim Davis—He's Got The World By The Tail" by Holly G. Miller

LIFE IN HELL/THE SIMPSONS

Comics Interview #74 (1989): An interview with Matt Groening by Mark Borax

Entertainment Weekly (May 19, 1990): "The Making Of *The Simpsons* "

Honk #3 (March 1987): "Confessions Of A Doodle God" by Kim Thompson

The Los Angeles Times Magazine (April 29, 1990): "Bart Simpson's Real Father" by Joe Morgenstern

Mother Jones (Jan./Feb. 1991): "The Rehabilitation of Bart Simpson" by Sean Elder.

Newsweek (Sept. 28, 1987): "A Doodle God Makes Good" by Jennifer Foote

Newsweek (April 23, 1990): "At Home With TV's Newest Domestic Travesty"

Saturday Review (Feb. 4, 1985): "Drawing Board—Matt Groening" by Lisa Kinoshita

The Seattle Times (Oct. 1990): "The Simpsons, Man!" by Paul Andrews

USA Weekend (Nov. 30-Dec. 2, 1990): "Simpsons 'R' Us!" compiled by Gayle Jo Carter

Boring, But Necessary Ordering Information!

Payment:

All orders must be prepaid by check or money order. Do not send cash. All payments must be made in US funds only.

Shipping:

We offer several methods of shipment for our product. Sometimes a book can be delayed if we are temporarily out of stock. You should note on your order whether you prefer us to ship the book as soon as available or send you a merchandise credit good for other goodies or send you your money back immediately.

Postage is as follows:

Normal Post Office: For books priced under $10.00—for the first book add $2.50. For each additional book under $10.00 add $1.00. (This is per indidividual book priced under $10.00. Not the order total.) For books priced over $10.00—for the first book add $3.25. For each additional book over $10.00 add $2.00.(This is per individual book priced over $10.00, not the order total.) These orders are filled as quickly as possible. Shipments normally take 2 or 3 weeks, but allow up to 12 weeks for delivery.

Special UPS 2 Day Blue Label Rush Service or Priority Mail(Our Choice). Special service is available for desperate Couch Potatoes. These books are shipped within 24 hours of when we receive the order and should normally take 2 to 3 days to get from us to you.

For the first RUSH SERVICE book under $10.00 add $5.00. For each additional 1 book under $10.00 add $1.75. (This is per individual book priced under $10.00, not the order total.)

For the first RUSH SERVICE book over $10.00 add $7.00 For each additional book over $10.00 add $4.00 per book.(This is per individual book priced over $10.00, not the order total.)

Canadian shipping rates add 20% to the postage total.

Foreign shipping rates add 50% to the postage total.

All Canadian and foreign orders are shipped either book or printed matter.

Rush Service is not available.

DISCOUNTS!DISCOUNTS!

Because your orders keep us in business we offer a discount to people that buy a lot of our books as our way of saying thanks. On orders over $25,00 we give a 5% discount. On orders over $50.00 we give a 10% discount. On orders over $100.00 we give a 15% discount. On orders over over $150.00 we giver a 20 % discount.

Please list alternates when possible.

Please state if you wish a refund or for us to backorder an item if it is not in stock.

100% satisfaction guaranteed.

We value your support. You will receive a full refund as long as the copy of the book you are not happy with is received back by us in reasonable condition. No questions asked, except we would like to know how we failed you. Refunds and credits are given as soon as we receive back the item you do not want.

Please have mercy on Phyllis and carefully fill out this form in the neatest way you can. Remember, she has to read a lot of them every day and she wants to get it right and keep you happy! You may use a duplicate of this order blank as long as it is clear. Please don't forget to include payment! And remember, we love repeat friends.

COUPON PAGE

_____Secret File: The Unofficial Making Of A Wiseguy $14.95 ISBN # 1-55698-256-9

_____Number Six: The Prisoner Book $14.95   ISBN# 1-55698-158-9

_____Gerry Anderson: Supermarionation $14.95

_____Calling Tracy $14.95 ISBN# 1-55698-241-0

_____How To Draw Art For Comicbooks: Lessons From The Masters

ISBN# 1-55698-254-2

_____The 25th Anniversary Odd Couple Companion $12.95   ISBN# 1-55698-224-0

_____Growing up in The Sixties: The wonder Years $14.95   ISBN #1-55698-258-5

_____Batmania $14.95   ISBN# 1-55698-252-6

_____The Year Of The Bat $14.95

_____The King Comic Heroes $14.95

_____Its A Bird, Its A Plane $14.95   ISBN# 1-55698-201-1

_____The Green Hornet Book $14.95

_____The Green Hornet Book $16.95 Edition

_____The Unofficial Tale Of Beauty And The Beast $14.95   ISBN# 1-55698-261-5

_____Monsterland Fear Book $14.95

_____Nightmare On Elm Street: The Freddy Krueger Story $14.95

_____Robocop $16.95

_____The Aliens Story $14.95

_____The Dark Shadows Tribute Book $14.95   ISBN#1-55698-234-8

_____Stephen King & Clive Barker: An Illustrated Guide $14.95 ISBN#1-55698-253-4

_____Drug Wars: America fights Back $9.95 ISBN#1-55698-259-3

_____The Films Of Elvis: The Magic Lives On $14.95   ISBN#1-55698-223-2

_____Paul McCartney: 20 Years On His Own $9.95   ISBN#1-55698-263-1

_____Fists Of Fury: The Films Of Bruce Lee $14.95   ISBN# 1-55698-233-X

_____The Secret Of Michael F Fox $14.95   ISBN# 1-55698-232-1

_____The Films Of Eddie Murphy $14.95   ISBN# 1-55698-230-5

_____The Lost In Space Tribute Book $14.95   ISBN# 1-55698-226-7

_____The Lost In Space Technical Manual $14.95

_____Doctor Who: The Pertwee Years $19.95   ISBN#1-55698-212-7

_____Doctor Who: The Baker Years $19.95   ISBN# 1-55698-147-3

_____The Doctor Who Encyclopedia: The Baker Years $19.95   ISBN# 1-55698-160-0

_____The Doctor And The Enterprise $9.95   ISBN# 1-55698-218-6

_____The Phantom Serials $16.95

_____Batman Serials $16.95

MORE COUPON PAGE

_____Batman And Robin Serials $16.95

_____The Complete Batman And Robin Serials $19.95

_____The Green Hornet Serials $16.95

_____The Flash Gordon Serials Part 1 $16.95

_____The Flash Gordon Serials Part 2 $16.95

_____The Shadow Serials $16.95

_____Blackhawk Serials $16.95

_____Serial Adventures $14.95   ISBN#1-55698-236-4

_____Trek: The Lost Years $12.95   ISBN#1-55698-220-8

_____The Trek Encyclopedia $19.95   ISBN#1-55698-205-4

_____The Trek Crew Book $9.95   ISBN#1-55698-257-7

_____The Making Of The Next Generation $14.95   ISBN# 1-55698-219-4

_____The Complete Guide To The Next Generation $19.95

_____The Best Of Enterprise Incidents: The Magazine For Star Trek Fans $9.95
                                                        ISBN# 1-55698-231-3

_____The Gunsmoke Years $14.95   ISBN# 1-55698-221-6

_____The Wild Wild West Book $14.95   ISBN# 1-55698-162-7

_____Who Was That Masked Man $14.95   ISBN#1-55698-227-5